Saint Peter's University Library
Withdrawn

This book tells how to
take your child out of public school

And how to educate him at home yourself.

It tells how to put your own school together
which means
legalities, curriculum, and business stuff

And about minding the store once you've started.

It tells about solutions for when you're in trouble . . .

But it does not flirt with dreams for an easy Utopia.

NO MORE
PUBLIC SCHOOL

H. BENNETT

RANDOM HOUSE — THE BOOKWORKS

Copyright © by Harold Zina Bennett 1972
All rights reserved under International and Pan-American Copyright Conventions.

First Printing February 1972,   2,500 copies hardcover
                                 15,000 copies paperbound

Cover design by Anne Kent Rush
Book design and illustrations by Linda Bennett
Cover photo of Sean McCrary by John Pearson
Typeset by Vera Allen Composition Service, Hayward, California
Printed and bound by The Book Press, Brattleboro, Vt.

This book is co-published by   Random House Inc.
                                  201 East 50th Street
                                  New York, N.Y. 10022

                         and   The Bookworks
                                  1409 Fifth Street
                                  Berkeley, California

Published in the United States, and simultaneously in Canada by Random House
of Canada Limited, Toronto.

Acknowledgement:
Special thanks to Frank James, Attorney at Law, who wrote the Articles of
Incorporation and the By-Laws that appear in the FORMS AND DOCUMENTS
section of this book.

ISBN: 0-394-48040-6 Tr.
Library of Congress Catalog Card Number: 71-39059

Random House – The Bookworks books are edited and designed in Berkeley and
produced in New York.

Manufactured in the United States of America.

.

THIS BOOK IS FOR PEOPLE WHO:

don't like the public schools and think they have no alternative

OR

teach in public schools

OR

are thinking about making their own school

OR

have a school going and are looking for tools to continue, improve, or expand their operation

OR

are curious members of the CIA, the State Department of Education, the PTA or other subversive organizations

My purpose is neither to romanticize nor to complain, but to make it possible for people with little or no previous experience to build realistic alternatives to the public school system.

THIS BOOK IS

This book tells all you need to know in order to:

- Take your child out of public schools legally or otherwise
- Set up a plan for the home instruction of your child
- Choose a more complex educational plan, such as:
  a. a Neighborhood Co-op School
  b. a Storefront School
  c. a big Private School
  d. a Mobile School
  e. a Trek-Around-The-Country School
  f. other more Exotic Ventures
- Set up a curriculum for:
  a. one child
  b. a few children
  c. any number of children
- Establish your group as an "approved" private school
- Establish your school as a legal corporation
- Establish your school as a non-profit, tax-exempt organization for the purpose of
  a. becoming eligible to receive Government Surplus property
  b. offering a tax deduction to anyone contributing money or materials to the school
  c. qualifying for lower fees for local licenses
  d. reducing required payroll deductions should you hire other people to work in the school
- Set up the business end of the school operation, meaning
  a. Daily routines
  b. Bookkeeping records
  c. Fee collections
  d. Payroll
  e. Cost of overhead
- Interview:
  a. Parents
  b. Students
  c. Teachers
  d. Authorities

- Survive in spite of conflicts with
  a. Neighbors
  b. Authorities
  c. Parents
  d. Students
  e. Comrades
- Choose a leader
- Keep going after the first year and in the face of
  a. divisions of loyalties
  b. differences of opinion among members on how and what to teach
- Get help when you need it, and learn how to ask for help

THIS BOOK IS NOT

This book will not give you reasons for taking your child out of the public schools, or reasons justifying the existence of new schools, so if you're at the place where you still need reasons, I suggest you read the following books:

1. *Crisis In The Classroom*, Charles Silberman, Vintage, $2.45
2. *Compulsory Mis-education, and The Community of Scholars*, Paul Goodman, Vintage $1.95
3. *The Politics of Schools, A Crisis In Self-Government*, Robert Bendiner, N.A.L. $1.95
4. *Death At An Early Age*, Jonathan Kozal, Bantam, $1.25
5. *Deschooling Society*, Ivan Illych, Harper & Row, $6.95
6. *How Children Fail*, John Holt, Dell, $. 95
7. *36 Children*, Herbert Kohl, Signet, $ .95
8. *The Way It Spozed To Be*, James Herndon, Bantam, $ .95
9. *Schools Where Children Learn*, Joseph Featherstone, Liveright, $2.45
10. *The Challenge of Youth*, Erik Erikson, DD Anchor, $1.95

TABLE OF CONTENTS

1

HOW TO TAKE YOUR CHILD OUT OF PUBLIC SCHOOL

BREAKING LOOSE

Compulsory Education means that your child must be in school. But there are a number of ways to take your child out of public school and avoid hassles with the authorities too. In the past few years parents have learned to do this in the following ways:

- take your child out of public school and tell the school authorities that you are moving to another state
- take your child out of public school and tell the school authorities that you are enrolling him in a private school
- never register your child in public school in the first place
- tell the authorities that you are starting a school of your own, then put together a school on paper only

Each of these ways is explored in detail in the pages that follow.

After you've taken your child out of public school you can:

- do nothing more
- educate your child at home yourself — or with a little help from your friends
- put your child in an existing private school
- make your own school with as many students and teachers as you want.

How to do each of these is explained in the following pages.

LAWS IN CALIFORNIA AND ELSEWHERE

Although my focus in this book will be on California laws, I will tell you as I go along how to get more specific information on laws in your own state. In many cases California is looser, in other cases it's tighter, than other states. For this reason, if no other, California law works well as a reference point from which to proceed, no matter what state you live in.

HERE'S HOW I DID IT

In California there are no official documents to sign to take your child out of public school. It does not matter, either, whether you take your child out in January or June or December. Why not take him out today?

Four days before I took my son out of school, I wrote this letter:

> My name
> address
> date

Dear ————,
Beginning on (date), my child, (name) will no longer be attending (name) School. At that time we plan to enroll him in a private school.

> Yours truly,
> (my signature)

I sent off two copies, one to the principal of my child's school, the other to his teacher.

If you want to avoid hassles with the authorities, you'll do the same. Here's why:

When the school officials get the letter in their files, they can write *DR* in the column on their attendance records that asks "Reason for Non-attendance." *DR* means *dropped*.

As long as the student's name appears on the school records, teachers will ask questions: "I wonder what happened to Johnny? Illness? Moved away? Family problems? Maybe dead?" Your letter will put an end to these questions, and will prevent referral of your "case" to the truant officer. Remember, moving away, and attendance in a private school are both legitimate reasons to take your child out of public school.

GETTING LOCAL INFORMATION

If you are living in another state, or you want to check up on local policies for taking your child out of the public school, do this:

Telephone the district Superintendent of School. You will
find his number listed in the telephone directory. Ask to talk
with the person who handles "attendance records." His title
is usually "Attendance Supervisor."

Here's what you say:

"Hello, I'm (name), and my child is attending the (name)
School. We are going to be sending our child to a private
school in (date). Are there any particular forms which your
office requires us to fill out when we take him out of the
public schools?"

If it turns out that there are forms to fill out, ask where to get them and
what you must do to process them. This kind of information is standard
procedure, and they will be glad to assist you.

DON'T EVER GIVE THEM YOUR NAME

In Paul Goodman's novel, *The Grand Piano* the hero, who systematically plays
truant, says, "Don't ever give them your name. Once they get your name they
own you."

If you were never to register your child in public school, when he came to
be kindergarten age the school authorities would have no way of tracing you.
Consider the thousands of children in Parochial schools who have never
registered with the public school authorities. You would be more or less free
of school hassles forever if you did that.

I know of one family in San Francisco who simply never registered. The
only problems they ran into occurred when they took the child to public
places during school hours. Sometimes strangers, usually old ladies, came up
and asked why the child was not in school. The mother developed a technique
for putting them off. She whispered to the stranger, "Birth defects. They
won't take her." This caused an embarrassed hush. But for those who pursued
the question further, the mother was always quick to reply, "I'd rather not
talk about it if you don't mind." It worked.

TAKING YOUR CHILD OUT OF SCHOOL THE WRONG WAY

Parents do get into trouble for taking their children out of school. But I have
never heard of a parent getting hassled after giving clear notification to the
authorities that they were taking their child out of public school in order to
put him in a private school, or because they were moving.

A friend of mine took her child out of the second grade, and did not say
anything to the school authorities about why she was doing so. Two or three
months later, she got a call from the teacher asking why the child was not in

school. The mother answered that she would not send the child to school because the child was too bored by it. The teacher reported what the mother had said to the principal, and the principal called the parent in for a conference. The parent didn't go to the conference, and the juvenile authorities were notified. The juvenile authorities came to my friend's house and told her that what she was doing was illegal.

There were threats of legal actions, but nothing happened for several months. Finally a summons was served to my friend. Two weeks before her court appearance, she enrolled her child in a private school. In court she stated that she had enrolled her child in a private school, and the case was dropped. A month later she took her child out of private school, too, and never heard from the authorities again.

GETTING AWAY

If you have already registered your child with the school people, consider moving to a different school district or a different town. First notify your present school that you are moving. Tell them that you're going to a different state, since they will want to transfer the child's records if your new address is close by. Then after you move don't register with the school in your new neighborhood. This is nearly as good as not registering in the first place.

You can, of course, tell them that you're moving away and then not move, just to get your child's name cleared. But then there's the chance that one of your child's old teachers will bump into you in the super market or somewhere and ask embarrassing questions. If you don't plan to move, it's better that you tell them your child is going to a private school. The explanations can come much easier, should you bump into your child's old teacher somewhere.

PEOPLE ASK QUESTIONS

If your child is out on the streets during the school hours, he has a chance of being seen and stopped by curious school people: teachers on their way back to work from dental appointments, conscientious cops, social workers, and clergymen.

You should thus keep your child off the streets during school hours, or figure out a plan for dealing with all such eventualities. You can figure out things to tell the authorities when and if they ask you what you're doing. But before getting into all that remember that you will probably have to teach your child to lie and be deceiptful. Ask yourself if you want this before you get wholly into it. Developing an elaborate defense will guarantee your own paranoia.

HOW TO PICK A PRIVATE SCHOOL

Now let's consider putting your child in an existing private school. There are two kinds of private schools to consider:

- approved private schools
- non-approved private schools

An approved school is one that is duly registered with the authorities. (See page 9 for how to do this.) A non-approved school is one which is not registered with the authorities: i.e., an *underground* school. (see page 30)

But remember, approval or non-approval of a school by the authorities will not determine that the school is or isn't a good place for children. There are bad approved schools just as there are good non-approved ones, and vice versa, of course.

In the eyes of the authorities, sending your child to an approved private school is just as acceptable as sending him to a public school. You will never tangle with the compulsory education laws if your child is enrolled in an approved private school.

The compulsory education laws do not specify which approved private school your child must attend. If you cannot find or afford a private school you will accept, or if you really don't care to try, you can set one up for yourself. That's what this book is about.

If you put your child in a non-approved school, do so with the knowledge that you are violating the compulsory education laws in the same way that you would be doing if you did not have your child in school at all. Depending on the community you live in, the authorities may do one or more of the following:

- avoid you so they won't have to do anything about you
- fine you
- slap a child neglect complaint on you, which can mean that they will assign a social worker or probation officer to your case in order to make certain that you educate your child in the "proper manner"
- just warn you

Most likely, they'll do the latter. Rap with people in your community who have had experience with this, and find out what the specific risks will be.

PAPER SCHOOLS

Some people in California file the necessary papers with the state to become recognized as a private school (see page 24). Then they do nothing more to meet state or local standards. If authorities ask where their children are, the paper school people say that they're in the process of putting together a private school — which is properly registered with the state — and the children are registered in that school. Most paper school people do keep attendance, since that's one of the big concerns of the public school people who come around to ask questions. (See page 15 for attendance records.)

In California, all private schools which have once filed their papers with the state will receive renewal notices the following year. Paper school people who know they can't meet local or state standards send the renewal back with the comment that they've gone out of business.

Understand that the authorities will buy the idea that you are teaching your child at home, or elsewhere, while you put together your school. But they won't go along with it for much more than a year. So the paper school people have their friends file new papers, with new names for the new school year. With a dozen parents co-operating, you can get through all twelve grades this way.

The intent here is not always to evade the authorities, but to have a way of gathering resources for a legitimate school operation. It is a way of doing this in a leisurely fashion. More than one parent group began this way, and went on to bigger things. It's just one way of getting your kid out of public school immediately and doing so in a way that will protect you from clear cut violations of the compulsory education laws.

(See pages 7-17 for instructions on how to file the papers for an approved private school.)

CONCLUSION

With the above information, anyone who wants to take his child out of public school can do it tomorrow. You now have two important tools in your hands:
- How to take your child out of public school with absolute minimum hassle from the authorities
- How to obtain the protection of an "approved" private school for at least one year, in the form of the "paper" school

All the methods described in this chapter have been tried, and are working for others. There's no reason they won't work for you.

2

MAKE A PAPER SCHOOL

GETTING STARTED

You'll need to familiarize yourself with the Compulsory Education Laws and with that section of your state's Education Code which deals with private education. The relationship between these two areas of law is relatively simple, explained as follows:

Although the Compulsory Education Laws generally state that all children between the ages of six and sixteen must attend a full-time day school, they do not specify which school the child must attend. You can satisfy the requirements of the law by having your child in a private school which meets the standards specified for private schools in the State Education Code.

Rather than try to deal with the Education Codes of every state in the Union, I have chosen to use the California Education Code as a reference point. There are a couple of reasons for doing this: the first is that I have dealt with the California codes myself, and am most familiar with them. But in addition, I recently learned that at least three other states have in the past year requested copies of the California codes dealing with private education, apparently because they had no guidelines of their own, and are themselves using the California codes as a model.

IF YOU LIVE OUTSIDE CALIFORNIA

If you are a resident of another state, look over what I have written on the California codes and then go to the nearest big city library and study what your own State Education Code says. The State code books are available to the public, and can be gotten at the reference desk of the bigger libraries. Ask to see the Education Codes, then study the index, tracing down anything that has "private school" or "private education" as part of its title. If you prefer, write to your State Department of Education and ask them to tell you what you must do to establish an approved private school. Do your letter like this:

> State Department of Education
> Capitol City, Your state
>
> Gentlemen:
>
> A group of parents and educators, of which I am one, are in the process of exploring the possibilities of setting up a private school for children between the ages of six and sixteen.
>
> Could you send us, or direct us to, sections of the State Education Code which contain laws or guidelines pertaining to the establishment and maintenance of private schools? We would also like to receive whatever forms and documents we must fill out to be duly registered with you as an approved institution.
>
> We thank you for your assistance.
>
> Yours truly,
> (your signature)

My experience with the bureaucracy has been that if you are specific and talk their language, you'll get what you need. I sent three letters to the same office before I got everything that I needed from the State Department of Education in California. The first letter got me a reply directing me to the State Education Code. The second letter got me a printed summary of the private education section of the state code. The third letter got me duplicates of what they'd already sent me plus a set of the forms and documents necessary for registering our school with them. Conclusion? Use the third letter, which is the one printed above. Copy it verbatum from the book, changing only names and addresses as necessary. The letter should be neatly typed. Call the Superintendent of Schools in your town to get the proper address and titles in your state.

All these details may. begin to sound nit-picky, and I agree with you that they are. But remember, the less energy spent hassling with the authorities, the more energy you will have for the more important business of running the school.

If you really want to keep your operation small, say five to eight children, or even if you plan to teach your own child at home, this information will be important to you. Knowing what the law says — which is what you learn by reading the education code — will be a valuable tool if and when you have to deal with the authorities. It will tell you what questions they are likely to ask, and thus arm you with acceptable answers.

HOW TO FILL OUT THE AFFIDAVIT

Turn to page 117 in Forms and Documents, and you'll find something called "Private School Affidavit." This affidavit is the foundation of your school; without it you have nothing as far as the authorities are concerned. If you start operating a school and you fail to file the affidavit, you will not be an "approved" school, and can be found in violation of the compulsory education laws.

Use a typewriter to fill out this form, preferably a machine with "elite" type face. Most government documents are designed to fit this smaller type face. The more businesslike you can be in the red tape department, the better the authorities will like it. Make it easy for them to process your papers smoothly. The benefit will be yours. The affidavit should be filled out in duplicate: one for them, and one for you.

Here are some points to follow in filling out this form:

I. School Names and Addresses

Decide on a name for the school. In choosing this name, remember that you do not want to draw negative attention to yourself. And here's why: in California, all registered private schools have their names and addresses recorded in a directory which goes out to local officials and anyone else who requests a copy. It might be true in your state too. If you call your school something like the *Fukutu Academy* you will be asking for trouble. Such names will antagonize every public officer in the county, as well as the local P.T.A., and they will probably dedicate the rest of their lives to closing you down. Choose a name that you can live with comfortably.

If your school is going to be the kind that meets in parks and public places, but has no building where you meet regularly, list the address where your records are kept. If you are doing a co-operative thing with parents teaching their kids in their own home, but meeting occassionally in public places, do not list the separate names and addresses of each co-operator. List only that address where your records are kept, and from which you do most of your business. (I will deal with the various kinds of schools in the chapter called "Models For Your Own School.")

II. Directors and Principal Officers

List at least two names and addresses here. The officers may be from the same family. For example, the husband and wife of one family might be

named as Director, and Educational Director. Here are some sample titles to choose from:
- Director
- Assistant Director
- Educational Director
- Secretary/Treasurer

The Educational Director is one of the key people. It is best to get someone to take this title who is either a credentialed teacher or a person with two or more years of teaching experience in schools either public or private. (See page 14 for more details.)

III. School Records

There are three kinds of records that you must keep for the school authorities. These are:
- Attendance (see page 14)
- A list of the courses your school offers, which conforms to the education code requirements (see page 15)
- Names, addresses, and educational backgrounds of each faculty member

Keep these records together. They should always be accessible, and kept up to date. Establish a place to keep them, and assign the responsibility for the records to one person.

In filling out the affidavit, the "Location address" means the address where the records are kept. More details on records will be given later in the book.

IV. Certification

The affidavit should be signed by the person listed in section II of the affidavit as the director of your school.

Page two of the affidavit begins with:

Private School Directory Data

The directory they're talking about here is a list of the names and addresses of all private schools in the state. These directories are available to all public officials, and to anyone else requesting one. Actually, the directory is a nice thing to have, since you may find some neighbors in it doing the same thing that you're doing, and you might get together with them and share resources, like each others' moral support. To get the California directory, send a dollar, along with a letter requesting "the current Private School Directory" to:

Fiscal Office, Order Section
California State Department of Education
721 Capitol Mall
Sacramento, California 95814

People in other states might also be interested in this directory, since it's a good way to find someone who's doing a school already; find a pen pal.

Paragraphs 1 through 8 of page 2 of the affidavit are self-explanatory. The only thing I might mention is under the second column, called:

Enrollment on October 1

If this form is being filled out for the first time, (i.e., if your school is just starting) type in the words "Please see enclosure," directly under the column subtitle. Then enclose the following message, typed on a separate sheet of paper:

> ENCLOSURE
>
> RE: Enrollment on October 1
> Number of pupils in each grade
>
> This is our first year of operation, and our enrollment is not yet stable. We are equipped to handle (number) pupils in grades one through six.

Attach this note to the back of the affidavit before you send it in.

SOME THINGS TO REMEMBER

As you're filling out the affidavit, list at least one teacher for every 25 kids. Understand that these do not need to be "credentialed" teachers, but at least one person on your staff should be. (see page 14) These points apply to page 1, paragraph II, page 2, paragraph 6, and page 2, "Enrollment on October 1."

The last section of page 2, called "Special Education" will apply only if you are running a school specifically for physically or mentally exceptional kids. That gets into a whole other set, and one I don't take on in this book. So if you're doing a regular school, just draw a diagonal line through this section to indicate that it doesn't apply to you.

FILING THE AFFIDAVIT AFTER OCTOBER 1–15

The state requires you to file the Private School Affidavit between October 1 and October 15 of each year. That's so they can make up the "Private School Directory," and they can't insert new listings past that date. But you might want to begin your school in January or some other time than October. Here's what to do:

Draft a letter which contains the same information asked for on page 1 of the affidavit, plus an explanation of the grade levels you'll be teaching. Explain to them that your school began accepting students after October 15, and tell them that you would like to receive an affidavit for the following year. In California, send this to:

> Bureau of Administrative Research and District Organization
> Department of Education
> 721 Capitol Mall
> Sacramento, California 95814

You will get a letter from them which will include a Private School Affidavit to fill out, or will explain that you cannot be listed in the current year's directory, or both. Their letter might also tell you to request an affidavit from your local Department of Education. They'll give you the address.

WHAT TO DO WITH THE AFFIDAVIT

The present procedure in California is for the local Department of Education to mail out the affidavits for the state. Likewise, you return the completed affidavit to the local people so that they can transmit the information to the state people. They will send you directions on how to do this.

If for some reason you are mailed an affidavit from the state people, fill it out and do this: (unless otherwise directed by them)

Prepare a packet containing the following:
- a copy of the affidavit
- a cover letter as follows:

> Your local Superintendent of Schools
> His address
>
> Dear , ——————,
>
> In compliance with the State Education Code, Section 29009.5, (California only) we are sending you the enclosed materials. A similar packet has been sent to the state.
>
> Should you wish any further information, I can be reached by telephone at ——— - ————.
>
> Yours truly,
> (your signature)

Before you send off the original affidavit, make up xerox copies for your own files. The same goes for any correspondence that you have with school authorities.

YOUR INVOLVEMENT WITH OTHER AUTHORITIES

Depending on how conspicuous you become, you will also be involved with one or more of the following agencies in your community:
- Health Department
- Fire Department
- Welfare Department (but only if you have students under the ages of 4 years 9 months)
- County Clerk's Office (through which the zoning board and business license people work)

Local policies will vary on this, and your involvement with other agencies will, in most cases, occur only after you rent or own a building. (See page 75)

Other ways to become conspicuous are to advertise in local newspapers, and to get publicity in a local newspaper column or feature article. Unless you're prepared to deal with all comers, shun this publicity. If, on the other hand, you're the kind of school that meets in public places only, or if you are just starting out with no more than one or two children other than your own in your own home, the authorities won't be very interested in you.

To find out what these people will expect of you, do this:

- Look up the addresses of each of the above agencies under your city and county listings in the phone book
- Write each of the agencies the following letter:

> Agency Name
> Address
>
> Gentlemen:
>
> A group of parents and teachers, of which I am one, are in the process of exploring the possibilities for establishing a private school. This school will be registered with the state department of education, in compliance with the Education Code.
>
> Can you advise us of the requirements of your agency regarding the operation and maintenance of a private school serving children between the ages of (number) and (number) years of age?
>
> At present we have no building, but will be interested in whatever advice you can give us in this regard.
>
> We thank you for your interest and co-operation.
>
> Yours truly,
(signature)

The agencies you'll be dealing with usually have printed materials stating their requirements as they will apply to you. Read these materials carefully when you get them. They will be especially important to you if you are considering signing a lease for classroom space (See page 125).

If there are any other private schools in your community, contact them and ask about their experience with county agencies. This information will be valuable to you. I have a friend who leased a building for his school and ended up having to put out $2,200 in order to bring it up to code. Don't make the same mistake.

THE CALIFORNIA EDUCATION CODE

On page 117, under Forms and Documents, you'll find a complete reprint of a bulletin put out by the California Department of Education, called "SUMMARY OF CERTAIN OF THE LAWS OF CALIFORNIA RELATING TO

THE ESTABLISHMENT AND MAINTENANCE OF PRIVATE SCHOOLS, PARTICULARLY THOSE OF KINDERGARTEN, ELEMENTARY AND SECONDARY GRADES." Yes, that's its actual title.

This summary is well detailed, but it's a drag to read. It contains information such as what you should put in your required First Aid Kit, what you should teach in the way of Health, and Accident Prevention – tidbits like that. Learn to cherish this document; look upon it as a list of answers to the questions the authorities might someday ask you.

The following paragraphs analyze the main points of the "Summary," and tell you how the regulations will affect you: (Read the "Summary," page 117, first.)

- "Children who are being instructed in a private, full time day school, by *persons capable of teaching* shall be exempted" (This means exempted from compulsory attendance in public schools.)
- "Such schools shall . . . *offer instruction in the several branches of study* . . . taught in the public schools of the state."
- "The attendance of the pupils shall be kept by the private school in a register, and *the record of attendance shall indicate clearly every absence of the pupil from school for a half day or more* during each day that school is maintained during that year."

The italicized words in the above three enumerated paragraphs are the key words and phrases. Let's look at them point by point and discuss how they apply.

- ". . . by persons capable of teaching . . .": The position taken by the California courts in several test cases indicates that the officials do not necessarily look at "credentials" granted by the State in order to determine whether or not a person is capable of teaching in a private school. However, if it came to a showdown, I am sure that they would require evidence of some sort of background in teaching. The "Summary" says that the "standards to be used should be comparable to those required for public school teachers excepting only as to the holding of credentials."

  In my search to discover what "comparable standards" meant, I went to a teacher's employment agency. Since this agency deals with superintendents in twenty or more counties, I felt they were in a pretty good position to give an overall view of California hiring practices. The answer I got from them was that "most" superintendents require at least a B.A. It is common practice for counties with small revenues to hire teachers with less than a credential because they can get away with paying the non-credentialed teacher anywhere from $2,000 to $4,000 a year less than the credentialed teacher. The state allows this practice through something known as the "postponement" clause. "Postponement" means that a teacher working toward a degree, or working toward acquiring academic credits to qualify for a credential, can be hired for a period of up to two years, which under certain circumstances can be extended.

As for private school, the employment agency told me that many private schools hire teachers with as few as two years of college, and hire teacher aids with no educational requirements whatsoever. Other private school directors tell me that if the principal or director of the school is an experienced teacher with a B.A., the state leaves them alone.

The standards, it would seem, are deliberately kept loose in order to provide maximum flexibility for the varied needs of school officials throughout the state. But to be on the safe side, I suggest finding either a credentialed teacher, or a person with a college diploma and some experience or coursework in Education, and get him involved in your school in some capacity. As your *Educational Director*, he fills the bill as far as the state is concerned, and can be a good resource for you.

Remember, this person would not have to teach on a regular full-time basis, but could be available to you and your staff as a consultant, sort of a part time principal. There are many disillusioned teachers around, and you should have no trouble finding someone to fill the bill. If you're lucky, you can get him to volunteer. Otherwise, offer a small salary, in return for meeting with him two to four times per month. How to find such a person? (see page 20)

- "... offer instruction in the several branches of study ..." In California, there is general agreement that these are:
    a. **For Grades 1–6:** English, Math, Social Science, Science, Fine Arts, Health, Physical Education
    b. **For Grades 7–12:** Must offer, English, Foreign Language, Early California History, History dealing with oppressed minorities, Science, Math, Fine Arts, Applied Arts, Driver's training (from a book) and Physical Education.
    c. **Additional Subjects:** These fall in the area of health and public safety, and to quote from the "Summary" they are:
        Public safety and accident prevention at appropriate grade levels.
        The nature of alcohol, narcotics, restricted dangerous drugs, and dangerous substances.
        Fire prevention
        Protection and conservation of resources
        The effects of alcohol, narcotics, drugs, and tobacco upon the human body.
    In most cases, you will find ways to incorporate this stuff into other subjects in your school. Fire prevention is best handled by a field trip to the Fire Department, for the younger children.
- "... the record of attendance shall indicate clearly every absence of the pupil from school for a half day or more ..." This one is easy. Go to a large stationary or school supply store and purchase a "Teacher's

Attendance Record." They cost around a dollar. Inside, you'll find sheets of lined paper, with spaces for students' names and the five days of each week for a nine month period. Each day, you simply check off who's there, who's not there, and who was tardy. This record must be kept in a safe place since it is one of the records which you are required to maintain in order to fulfill the tenets of the Compulsory Education Laws. (see page 122)

KEEPING IN TOUCH WITH THE SYSTEM

Should you wish to keep in touch with what the public schools expect of children, you can get a publication known as the "Basic Course of Study." This is an outline of courses, and course content ordinarily taught in grades K–8 in California. In addition, it lists the books used in the public schools, and adopted by the State Board of Education. The State requires certain tests for measuring "academic achievement" at various grade levels. A list of these tests is enclosed. In the back of the "Basic Course of Study" is a small catalog of publications available for sale through twenty-two County Schools Departments.

The "Basic Course of Study" is available to private schools from most of the twenty-two California counties listed below. The price per copy ranges from 65¢ to about $2.00. To get a copy, call the County School Department nearest you, and get in touch with someone in the "Professional Library," or the "Curriculum Library," or the "Media Center" – called by different names in different places. These are the counties who have "Basic Course of Study" available:

Alameda	Marin	Santa Barbara
Calaveras	Mono	Santa Clara
Contra Costa	Monterey	Santa Cruz
Del Norte	Napa	Sierra
Humboldt	Placer	Sonoma
Inyo	San Benito	Trinity
Lake	San Joaquin	Ventura

If you're from out of state, or from a California county not listed here, contact the County Schools Department of Education in the county in which you live and explore what they have comparable to the "Basic Course of Study." If they have nothing, and you still want a copy of "Basic Course of Study," call Information for one of the counties listed above, and write or phone them. Here's what you might tell them:

I represent a private school, and we want to design our curriculum to parallel academic patterns of the public schools. Can you supply us with a copy of "Basic Course of Study," which I understand is an excellent guide for doing this?

You can assure yourself of absolute parallels between your own school curriculum and the public school curriculum by setting up a "testing" program. For more information on this, see page 99.

CONCLUSIONS

Once you file your Private School Affidavit, you may or may not hear from the school authorities again. In California, if you do, they will be interested in the following: (see page 89 for more details.)

- The names, addresses, and educational qualifications of each faculty member
- Attendance records on each student
- The courses of study offered

You will need to keep these records together and handy. The section of this book called "Who's Minding the Store," will tell you how to do this simply. In the meantime, you've done all you have to do to get started.

3

GET YOURSELF TOGETHER

HUMAN RESOURCES COME FIRST

If you've got children, a roof over your head, a handful of friends, and can raise fifty dollars, you've got all you need to start a school. Children do not need buildings, and desks, and principal's offices in order to learn. Learning can take place anywhere, in living rooms, parks, storefronts, and out on the street. Libraries, museums, and man's natural as well as created environments provide all the educational resources you'll ever need.

* * *

Focus on human resources. The greatest human resource is *interest*, since that's what provides positive energy. Spend time with yourself figuring out how much and what kinds of energy you have to give. If your interests run toward the business end of the school, don't get hung up teaching. And if teaching turns you on, let someone else do the business stuff.

* * *

Trust your gut feelings at this point, and be cautious of anything that seems to come from the head. The brain is a good tool, but seldom accurate for getting in touch with your interests.

* * *

Teaching children, coping with laws and business procedures, and getting in touch with gut feelings probably won't seem very compatible at first, so take your time with it. Remember, moving with your deepest interests will open the way for a positive flow of energy.

* * *

Understand that you will have to deal simultaneously with:

- Choosing a learning model, and establishing a curriculum for your child
- Establishing the legality of your school
- Conducting the business of the school
- Relating to other parents, children, agencies, business types, and comrades

The frequency, complexity, and depth of your involvement with the above ranges from about zero if you just pull your kid out of school, then do nothing, to maybe overwhelming if you try to establish a large free school right away.

* * *

If while you are doing all this planning you also have your child out of public school, remember that you will have to schedule time to spend with him.

* * *

Seek your own natural limits. Don't take on more responsibility than you can handle. Let other people share the load, or cut back your conception until it fits your natural limits.

STAY SMALL OR GET BIG

You may want to begin home instruction with your own child alone, and there's no reason that shouldn't be done. Many people have started with their own child at home, then have found other parents who took an interest in what they were doing; many such relationships have evolved into larger co-operative ventures. You'll see how this can work after you've read the section called MODELS FOR YOUR OWN SCHOOL.

Many other parents have chosen to keep their schools within the family unit, and have done so successfully.

When you come to parts in this book which seem to you to be dealing with something bigger than you want to get into, remember this: I wanted to keep this book as simple and compact as possible. For this reason, I often deal with a happy medium, a school of thirty children, the intent being to provide a model which can be easily adapted to work for everyone, from the smallest school (one student), to the largest (200?). The intent was not to suggest that everyone set his goals at making a school for thirty children or more.

For readers interested in the smallest school operation, turn right now to "A School In a Suitcase," (page 38) which will give you a better idea of just how simple and fun this whole matter of home instruction can be. Your models will be The Minimal School One, (page 24) and either a simplied version of What We Do All Day (page 41) or "Working by the Clock" (page 95). After looking these sections over, you will find that you can relax with the rest of the book.

GETTING IN TOUCH WITH OTHER PARENTS

You may feel that you're alone in your desire to make a school. Your friends, though sympathetic with your views, have no children of their own and so can't offer much more than moral support. So you need to get together with other parents like yourself. Here's what you can do:

Make a simple ad. It might go like this:

SCHOOL PROBLEMS?

Parents. Teachers. Are you interested in a small private school for children from five to twelve years old? Low or no tuition? Relaxed, open classroom. Let's get together. (Your name, address, and telephone number.)

Type the ad on a 4 x 5 or 5 x 7 index card. Make several to put up in super markets, laundromats, and other community bulletin boards. Or you can buy an ad in your favorite newspaper, listing the ad under "Business Personals" in more traditional newspapers.

Before the calls start coming in, schedule a date for a parent meeting about a month in the future. When people call you can explain what you're doing, and invite them to the meeting. This meeting will be a workshop for people wanting to start a school. (See Interviews, page 87.)

Use this book as the agenda for your meetings. Choosing the kind of school which will best meet your needs will be one of the first concerns, and that is covered under Models, page 23. From then on the order of business will look something like this:

- Who's going to file the papers with the authorities?
- Who's going to get the classroom stuff together?
- Who's going to take care of the files?
- Who's going to mind the store?
- Who's going to be the teacher?

ADVERTISING FOR A TEACHER

In many communities, disgruntled credentialed teachers are working at non-teaching jobs because they don't want to teach in the confining atmosphere of the public schools. However, many of these would gladly teach if they could find a less confining situation.

To get in touch with such teachers, make up an ad. Do it like this:

TEACHER WANTED

Small private school starting. Relaxed open classroom. For children from five to twelve. Contact: (your name, telephone)

Type the ad on index cards, the same as you did for getting in touch with parents. And put the cards up in the same places you put the ads for parents.

In addition to the index cards, and an ad in the newspaper, contact a college near you and ask to be put in touch with the "Student Employment Service." It may not be called that at the college you contact, but they will know what you mean.

Tell the "Student Employment Service" that you are starting a private school and that you want to hire a teacher. The employment people will probably have you come in and fill out some papers describing what you want. If you're not within driving distance of the college, ask them to mail you the papers. After the papers are filled out they'll put out feelers to help find the right person for you.

If you visit the college, take along several of those ads you typed on index cards, and put them up on bulletin boards wherever you can find space.

ADS IN SCHOOL MAGAZINES

New Schools Exchange, a magazine about schools with national distribution, prints a column called "Places Seeking People," and one called "People Seeking Places." You can advertise with them, or you can read their ads to find a teacher. Their address is:

NEW SCHOOLS EXCHANGE
301 E. Canon Perdido
Santa Barbara, Calif. 93103

A similar setup is offered for the Eastcoast/Midwest by *Outside the Net.* They call their column "Resources." Their address is:

OUTSIDE THE NET
P.O. BOX 184
Lansing, Michigan 48901

If you know of other such publications, by all means make use of them.

BOOKS ON HOW TO TEACH

Practical books on how to teach are difficult to find. There are thousands of books around which claim to be instructive, but which prove to be pretentious and abstruse. Don't be mislead by such books. Here are two which actually describe things to do.

- Piaget for Teachers, by Hans G. Furth, Prentice Hall $3.50
- Teaching As A Subversive Activity, Postman & Weingartner, Delta Books, 750 Third Ave., New York, N.Y. 10017, $2.25

Either or both of these will get you started into solid and creative teaching. But first, see page 92.

REFLECTIONS

Trust yourself. If you have the interest and energy to start a school, you can succeed. New ventures, and prospective changes always bring with them a certain amount of anxiety. You doubt that you can do something new simply because you've never done it before. That doubt is a common human experience. But don't let your doubts stop you from doing it. Remember, there are hundreds of people in the U.S. running schools right now, but who had never done it before. Their experience has created a field of energy for everyone to tap into. Join in now, and help expand this field. (to get a directory of "new" schools in the U.S. write New Schools Exchange, see page 21.)

It is estimated that there will be as many as 25,000 new schools started in the U.S. in 1972.

IS PRESCHOOL EDUCATION YOUR BAG?

This book does not get into the problems of *licensing* preschool programs: i.e., schools for kids younger than five years of age. Much of the information you'll find here will be helpful in the actual operation of such a school, but will not tell you anything about licensing per se.

In most cases, preschools are licensed by the Department of Social Welfare, and not by the Department of Education. So, if this is your concern, contact your local Social Welfare Department and ask to talk with someone about licensing a preschool program. They will tell you what you have to do. In addition, there's an abundance of excellent literature available on all aspects of setting up and running preschool programs. The best sources seem to be:

1. U.S. Department of Labor
   Women's Bureau
   Washington, D.C. 20210

2. Child Welfare League of America
   44 East 23rd Street
   New York, New York 10010

Write to either or both of these and ask them for their lists of publications having to do with Preschool Education and Daycare.

4

MODELS FOR YOUR OWN SCHOOL

GOING AHEAD

Let's assume now that you have taken your child out of public school, and that you have completed either the private school affidavit discussed here, or its equivalent in your state, and have sent it in to the authorities. You now have at least a year free of the public schools in which to do the following:

- Explore the possibility of educating your child yourself
- Establish your own private school
- Make a decision about which existing private school seems right for your child

You can begin by experimenting with one of the nine models detailed in this chapter. The models are called:

> THE NON-SCHOOL
> THE MINIMAL SCHOOL ONE
> THE MINIMAL SCHOOL TWO
> THE STOREFRONT SCHOOL
> THE BIG PRIVATE SCHOOL
> THE MOBILE CLASSROOM SCHOOL
> THE UNDERGROUND SCHOOL
> THE TREK AROUND THE COUNTRY SCHOOL
> THE MORE EXOTIC VENTURES

Your own needs and resources will dictate which model you follow.

THE NON-SCHOOL

- A non-school is:
  - a. a school on paper only: there are no classes
  - b. a system of keeping attendance and other records, in order to satisfy compulsory attendance regulations
  - c. a workable model for people who believe that the best school is no school at all
  - d. easily adapted for apprentice learning (see page 47)
- Get it started by:
  - a. getting together parents and students who are interested in this model
  - b. establishing the paper school (see page 7)
  - c. finding a credentialed teacher to act as principal-consultant (page 20)
- Keep it going by:
  - a. appointing one person to set up and keep records (see page 66)
  - b. setting up student records on each student "enrolled" (see page 67)
  - c. Keeping attendance records
  - d. establishing, on paper only, a schedule of classes to be held in various homes, public places, beaches, parks, etc. The schedule would follow state curriculum requirements (see page 117)
- Advantages would be:
  - a. complete flexibility for people to learn at their own rate and in their own style
  - b. that there would be no classes to attend
- Disadvantages would be:
    that the school would not stand up under close inspection in many states. (see page 117)

THE MINIMAL SCHOOL ONE

- A minimal School one is:
  - a. learning takes place in the home with parent as the teacher, and with certain areas of the home set aside as learning areas (see pages 33, 41, and 92.)
  - b. child works at learning basic skills for one or two hours per day: (see page 95)
      reading & writing skills
      mathematics
      social science: history, etc.
      science
      art

c. parent and child go on field trips, about three hours per week:
  — museums: natural science, history, art
  — to the building of a house, highway, large building, etc.
  — hardware store to explore tools and materials
  — library: study of books, public records, books of laws and how they affect the community; old newspapers; reference books; children's section
  — other schools to see what they're doing

d. child visits parents or friends at their work to get an idea of what adults do at their jobs away from home

e. child goes to park or somewhere else that he can play freely with children his own age for two hours per day at least

- Get started by:
  a. talk with your child about not being in public school, and about learning at home following this plan
  b. have the child help choose and set up the areas for study in the home, and take him along with you to buy supplies with which to equip the school
  c. put together the "School In a Suitcase" (page 38)

- Keep it going by:
  a. set up regular hours for the study periods each day
  b. keep your child off the streets during public school hours
  c. collect new materials to add to the work space (page 58) to keep the child's interest high

- Advantages would be:
  a. child would be learning at his own pace, and in his own style
  b. learning would become, for the child, an individualized and personal process rather than a large group process with very little personal meaning.

- Disadvantages would be:
  a. parent and child would be together for a great many hours each day
  b. parent would not have the "babysitting" service of the public schools
  c. would be in violation of compulsory education laws unless provisions were made to hire a credentialed teacher (page 13), and to put together the paper school (page 7).

THE MINIMAL SCHOOL TWO

- A minimal school two is:
    a. essentially an extension of the minimal school one, because several parents work together simultaneously
    b. parents can choose to teach each other's children
    c. parents may go together and hire a credentialed teacher to act as consultant and "principal" to the group. (see page 87)
    d. parents and children get together as a group for field trips, free play in parks or back yards, or for special events such as a movie in someone's home with a rented projector
- Get started by:
    a. evolving out of the minimal school one
    b. meeting with other parents to discuss the possibility of the plan
    c. putting together a paper school (see page 7)
    d. setting up areas in homes for learning
    e. making arrangements between parents for "trading" students, setting up field trips, and comparing resources, ideas, etc.
- Keep it going by:
    a. appointing one or more people to keep records
    b. appointing one or more people for minding the store (page 64)
    c. holding monthly group meetings to discuss problems and share revelations with each other
- Advantages would be:
    a. all those listed under minimal school one, plus
    b. parents and children would be able to share their experiences with other parents and children
    c. parents as teachers would be able to develop insight into their own children through teaching other children
- Disadvantages would be:
    a. parents would not have the "babysitting" service of the public school
    b. parents and children would be together most of the day.

THE STOREFRONT SCHOOL

- A storefront school is:
    a. the next logical step in the growth of your school
    b. takes place in a rented space (see page 75)
    c. suitable for fifteen to thirty children
    d. has at least one credentialed full-time teacher
    e. is supported by parents sharing total costs of maintaining the operation

- Get started by:
    a. evolving out of minimal school plans
    b. parents and teachers get together to discuss the plan
    c. setting up the paper school (see page 7)
    d. renting space and preparing cost estimates for divvying up expenses between the parents:
    >   Rent: about $150 per month
    >   Utilities: about $65 per month
    >   Insurance: about 20 per month
    >   Materials: about $25 per month
    >   Teacher's salary: $450 per month and up
    >   Other costs: $40 per month
- Keep it going by:
    a. appointing one or more people to mind the store (see page 64)
    b. building equipment for classrooms (see page 49)
    c. setting up work spaces in the classroom (see pages 33-40)
    d. holding monthly meetings with parents and staff (see page 85)
    e. setting up a non-profit corporation (see page 76)
- Advantages would be:
    a. relaxed open classroom environment (see page 41)
    b. children's daily involvement with others their own age
    c. parents would have time away from their children
    d. plan would satisfy compulsory education laws
- Disadvantages would be:
    a. cost of maintaining the school would be from $30 to $75 per month per child
    b. the problems of maintaining a complex organization (see pages 64, 81, and 98)
- Additional considerations:
    a. requires complex staffing:
        – teacher: one or more on a paid basis
        – janitor and maintenance: volunteer or paid
        – someone to mind the store: volunteer or paid
    b. requires involvement with people outside the school
        – fire and health department inspectors (see page 74)
        – city clerk's office: or zoning board, permit board (see page 13)
    c. size of rented space will in some ways determine how many students can be enrolled:
        – inside: minimum of 35 square feet per child
        – outside: ideally 75 square feet per child, or use a nearby park
    d. will involve transportation problems if trips away from school are planned

28

e. insurance must cover: (see page 69)
  – employees
  – liability and accidents
  – fire, theft, and vandalism

THE BIG PRIVATE SCHOOL

Most things will be pretty much the same as with the storefront school, except that all jobs will be more complex. The following list will help clarify this:

- You're big when you get over 30 kids.
- Recommended staff patterns are:
    a. Principal: 1 for any number up to 200 students
    b. Teachers: 1 for each group of 25 students or less
    c. Secretary: ½ time for up to 50 students; full-time for anything bigger
    d. Bookkeeper/payroll clerk: ¼ time for up to 50 students; ½ time up to 120 students; full-time for anything bigger
    e. Janitor/maintenance man: ½ time up to 35 students, full time for anything bigger
    f. Bus driver: full-time if transportation is to be provided for students to and from school. In this case, parents pay extra for transportation. Very expensive proposition. Most schools do best by contracting their transportation with private bus companies. Even many public schools find it more economical to do this.
- The larger the school, the more rigid are the inspections from:
    a. The Fire Department
    b. The Health Department
    c. The Building Inspectors/Zoning board
- You will definitely need the services of a lawyer in the event of lawsuits from:
    a. parents
    b. people with whom you contract work done
    c. visitors injured on the premises
- Utility costs: Gas, lights, trash, telephone:
    a. figure $2 per month per child in the summer
    b. figure $3 and up per month per child in the winter, depending on the climate
- Total insurance costs go up, but are less per individual covered.
- The larger you get, the more conspicuous you become to the community. You will be asked more questions, and will hear more complaints from outsiders in direct proportion to your size. Parents discuss their children's schools with their friends. Figure that each family has ten friends. Multiply that times fifty students. That's 500 outsiders who will

hear about your school. Since you'll have to spend a lot of time with public relations anyhow, consider assigning one person to this task. He will communicate what's going on at the school through newspapers, radio broadcasts, advertisements in the Yellow Pages of your phone book, and speaking engagements with local civic organizations.

- A large amount of capital will be involved, requiring:
  - a. the establishment of a corporation (see page 76)
  - b. careful record keeping (see page 64)
  - c. a board of directors, or other form of "steering committee" made up of stockholders, donors and patrons, parents, and loyal outsiders.
- A word of caution: YOU DAMNED WELL BETTER PLAY IT STRAIGHT WITH ALL PUBLIC AGENCIES.

THE MOBILE CLASSROOM

The important features of the mobile classroom are:
- mobility, which provides access to a wide variety of experiences
- stability of work spaces, which keeps personal belongings, materials, and tools within easy reach for everyone.

The mobile classroom is thus quite similar to the general operation of the storefront school, with mobility added. The following will help clarify this:
- Here's what you will need to do:
  - a. get a large school bus: a new 50 passenger model costs about $15 thousand; a descent used one can be found through the trucks ads in your newspaper for as little as $15 hundred, which is about what you'd pay for a year's rent on a storefront.
  - b. remove all but five or ten double seats, depending on the number of students you want to carry: limit to no more than 15 kids.
  - c. convert the open space in the back of the bus for work spaces, adapting the work space plan of page 33 to fit your bus. Keep everything compact.
- You'll need a teacher-driver, and one assistant.
- Bus will travel to places of interest, but will also provide familiar work spaces inside.
- Establish an itinerary, but keep it flexible. Start with trips which relate directly to subject matter being taught, then loosen up with trips which don't seem immediately relevant:
  - a. Subject-related trips include: a bank (Arithmetic), or a farm (Biology, Ecology, Geography), or a newspaper office (Reading and Writing).
  - b. Non-subject-related trips include: seashore, camping, fishing, watching a house being built.

Auto clubs often have maps showing points of historical interest. Once you get started many other possibilities will open up to you; mobility will lead to discovery. Note: Always phone anyone you're going to visit at least a week in advance, to ensure their co-operation.

- Travel itinerary would include:
    a. day trips as outlined under The Minimal School
    b weekend trips using bus as living space
    c. extended trips to other cities, states, countries
- Would require expensive insurance:
    a. Liability: $250 annually
    b. Medical: $5 per year per child
    c. Fire, theft, vandalism: $75 to $100 annually
- Potentially high maintenance costs
    a. Toll roads about four times that of auto
    b. Gasoline: five miles per gallon
    c. Tires: $45 and up per tire
    d. Tools for maintenance and repair: $85
    e. Valve job on engine: $400 and up
    f. Major overhaul of transmission: $250 and up
    g. New battery: $45 and up
    h. High license costs: $40 if registered as a "motor home" in California, to $1,000 per year if registered as a "commercial carrier." (Check with your Department of Motor Vehicles, or whatever.)
- Would expose children to a large variety of experiences offered by:
    a. the culture
    b. the natural environment
- Would not be hassled by inspectors from the Health Department, Zoning Board, etc.
- Would be practical only in the better climates.
- Over a period of years, the costs of maintaining the bus would probably be comparable to the costs of maintaining a building.

THE UNDERGROUND SCHOOL

- "Underground" means "deliberately avoiding the authorities." Reasons for an underground school include:
    a. You need a school situation for your child immediately, but putting together a "legal" school is still in the future
    b. You have had problems with the authorities for which there appear to be no solutions except this one
    c. You are on a political trip which requires that you elude all connections with all authorities
    d. You are on a paranoid trip and you like it that way
- I know of underground schools with as many as sixty students, mostly students of highly mobile families, who simply drop out of sight when things get hot.

- Underground schools sometimes rent buildings for their operation but they keep what they're doing a secret as much as possible. This means finding a building in which the school operation is not visible from the street. Consider warehouses or homes where the neighbors either can't see you or are sympathetic and won't cause you any hassles.
- "Floating" underground schools generally follow the patterns of THE MINIMAL SCHOOL ONE and TWO, but moving frequently, and before outsiders can ask any questions. They meet wherever there's space available: abandoned buildings, parks, and homes.
- The first principal of the Underground School is: NEVER TELL THE AUTHORITIES ANYTHING. Shun all publicity.
- Restrictions on schools for children over twelve years of age are fairly loose in California, making this model workable for that age group. (Check the Education Codes in your state.)

THE TREK AROUND THE COUNTRY SCHOOL

An increasing number of people live in Volkswagen buses, trucks converted to homes, and campers. They travel from place to place, making mobility their way of life. Some travel in groups, others alone. They eat, sleep, live and study on the road, stopping in one place for a number of days, weeks, or months when it's desirable.

Any family who does this for a few months, or a year, or more can incorporate a school into their plans by:

- Taking along a "School In A Suitcase" (see page 38)
- Basing the school activities on Minimal School One (see page 24)
- Although in violation of the compulsory education laws, unless you happen to be a credentialed teacher, there's little chance of hassles with the authorities since:
    a. treking families are not identified with any particular community
    b. authorities who enforce compulsory education laws tend to watch over only the citizens from the community that pays their salaries
    c. when hassled by authorities, treking families simply tell them that they're on their way to settle in a town in another state

OTHER MORE EXOTIC VENTURES

Some people abandon all ties with tradition, and strike out on paths which few have previously travelled. Often, this involves learning an entirely new life style, something you don't do from reading books but only through the realities of *doing it*: encountering new experiences and learning how to handle new problems as they arise. Here are a few such examples:

- A husband and wife, plus their three children, equipped themselves as a horseback expedition and followed the Pacific Trek Trail System — a "wilderness trail" — from Mexico to Canada. For nearly a year they lived as our Western pioneers must have lived. (See "Life Magazine," Sept 3, 1971; feature article called, "A Family Clip Clops all the way from Mexico to Canada.")
- A California High School bought a surplus ferryboat in New York, made it shipshape, then brought it back to the West Coast via: St. Lawrence Seaway, around the Great Lakes to the mouth of the Mississippi River, down the river to the Gulf of Mexico, thus through the Panama Canal to the Pacific Ocean, and thus up the West Coast back to San Francisco Bay. Guided by their teacher, an ex-marine mechanic, the high school students lived on the boat and depended on the sea for most of their food.
- A commune of five families bought several large buses, converted them to work, learning, and living spaces. Traveling freely from one section of the country to another, teaching their children, manufacturing small craft items for sale, and the day-to-day business of living were incorporated into the whole. Daily routines (the chores) were divided among all the various members of the commune, with children participating as much as possible. Two adults assumed the job of teaching the children, and most of the "schooling" was carried on in one of the buses which had been equipped just for that purpose.
- A high school in California presently takes regular backpacking trips into the Sierras. These trips last for two to three weeks, and the students, guided by a man who knows how, learn how to "live off the land." They carry no food into the mountains, and they limit the content of their packs to the barest essentials. The trips augment a regular school program back in the city.

Any of these plans, as well as others you and your friends might invent, epitomize learning-by-doing. The actual process of learning how and what to do is education in its purest form. Let your imagination and ingenuity be your guide.

5

HERE'S WHAT A CLASSROOM LOOKS LIKE

WHAT IS A CLASSROOM?

A classroom is an arrangement of work spaces:

- Books
- Math
- How Things Fit Together
- Building Things
- Science and Nature
- Art
- Learning About Other People
- Outside Play
- Miscellaneous and Portables

Each work space is defined by the materials it contains. For example, the work space for Math would have: an abacus, rulers, measuring cups, a dozen fake eggs, etc. These would stand on an open shelf so that children could choose and work with them freely.

Close to the shelf is a work surface. This surface might be a table (Math), an easel (Art), or a pillow on a rug (Reading). The surface would be chosen for how it best worked with the subject related to it.

CHOOSING THE RIGHT WORK SURFACE

Remember to keep tables and chairs at a comfortable height for children. Chairs 14" high, tables 23" high for children 5 to 12 years old. Use standard adult size for older students.

Tables fifteen inches high, surrounded by soft padded rugs allow children to kneel, stand up, and move about freely as they work. This does away with stumbling against chairs, and the restrictive feeling of sitting in chairs, and allows the child a comfortable degree of large muscle activity while still giving him a focus on his work.

Low kneeling tables can be constructed from plywood ¾ of an inch thick by four feet square. This is exactly one half of a standard size sheet of plywood. Make legs from two by four material, nailed together in a simple "H" pattern. Use wood screws to fasten tops to legs. (see page 49 for construction details.)

You'll also need tables and chairs. When children are learning to write letters and numbers, which requires precise control of the small muscles in their fingers, they usually prefer the greater restrictiveness of the chair and table combination.

HERE IS A LIST OF WORK SPACES

- Space For Books
    - a. Work surface — large comfortable pillows, soft rug, one four foot square kneeling table
    - b. Open shelves for books and magazines

    Illustrated story books

    Books of maps

    Mail-Order catalogs

    Photography books

    Books of paintings

    Hotrod magazines, Mechanics Illustrated, National Geographics, Flying Magazine

    Books on space

    Illustrate "How To" books in carpentry, fixing cars, building boats, building houses, etc.

    Books on sex written for kids

    Illustrated Ecology Books

    Illustrated Encyclopedia

    Books on dinosaurs and animals

    A box of 5x7 index cards with one word on each card

    A shoebox full of 2 inch plastic or wood letters

    flashcards with words and pictures

- Math space
    - a. Work surface—table and chairs for four to six children
    - b. Shelves with simple materials

    Abacus

    Rulers

    Measuring cups

    Dominoes

    Dice

    A dozen fake eggs (make them by pouring plaster into hollowed-out egg shells)

    Scales for weighing in pounds

    Play money

    A box of 5x7 index cards with adding, subtracting, multiplying and dividing problems. One problem per card. Answers on backs.

    A box of beads of several different colors with strings, for teaching "sets"

- How Things Fit Together
  - a. Work surface — Kneeling Table
  - b. Shelves with materials

Checkers and checkerboard

Simple and complex puzzles

Small plastic, interlocking
building blocks (Leggos)

Pipe fittings (plumbing pipe)

Old clocks and motors to
take apart

Tinkertoys

- Building Things Space
  - a. Work Surface — Floor or Ground
  - b. Storage of materials will vary

Cardboard panels with holes punched on edges, to be fastened together by looping pipe cleaners of soft wire through the holes

Large wooden blocks cut from pine timbers, or driftwood collected from the seashore

Large sheets of canvas (6'x6') with grommeted corners for fastening to ground, chairs, etc., with ropes, stakes, and poles

- Science and Nature Space
  - a. Work Table for display, dissecting, etc.
  - b. Shelves for materials and aquariums

Live fish and turtles

Rocks, moss, leaves, and
fungus collected on
nature walks

A chemistry set

Glass bottles for collecting in-
sects on nature walks
(Masen jars with discs of fine
wire mesh replacing tin in-
serts are best)

Magnets and small pieces of
iron as well as non-con-
ducting metals

6 volt battery, light bulb,
bell, wire, switches, small
compass

A set of pulleys, and gears

Magnifying Glass

A set of mirrors and prisms

A microscope

- Art Space
  - a. Work surface

Easel

Table for drawing

Carpentry bench with tools,
wood, and nails

Clay table (standing up
height)

Chalk board

  - b. Shelves for supplies

Crayons

Brushes

Water colors

Paper for easel and crayon
drawing

Colored pencils

Felt tip pens (colored)

White glue

Old magazines for collage

  - c. Large display area along one wall, made of soft material such as "celotex," so that pictures can be fastened to it with thumb tacks

- Learning About Other People Space
  a. Work Area — Table and chairs, or table at kneeling height placed on soft rug
  b. Storage — large cardboard box, or "R-Kive" file box (purchase at stationary store for about $2.00) with file folders

    Photos of people from other places pasted on 8½ x 11 cardboard panels, cut from magazines or travel brochures.

    Photos of people doing things from same sources as above: farming, washing clothes in a stream, repairing a truck engine, doctoring, working in a factory, building a house or large building, running a train, operating a computer, walking on the moon, etc.

    Cut titles and short bits of information from text of magazines to paste to the back of the pictures (Remember, old magazines are free. So is cardboard.)
- Space for Outside Play
  a. Wheel toys such as wagons or trikes and bicycles if there's a good hard surface for them
  b. Play house made of scrap lumber
  c. Rope swing with old tire if there's a good tree for it
  d. Heavy knotted rope for climbing if there's a tree for it
  e. Portable swing equipment if there's no tree
  f. Ten or fifteen old tires to stack and climb inside of
  g. Wading pool or sprinkler for hot days
  h. A small garden if there's space for it
- Miscellaneous and Portables
  a. Several clip boards with pads of lined paper for working out problems in reading, writing, arithmetic, etc. Suggest each child get one for himself, with his name painted in large letters on the back. Provide a place to hang them.
  b. Pencils, erasers, ball point pens, and felt-tipped marking pens for everyday use
  c. A mobile of the solar system to hang from the ceiling (can be cut from cardboard, hung with strings and coat hanger wire
  d. A file of "free literature." Collect such things as:

    Directions from games

    Clippings from magazines on how to do things such as repairing bikes, building toys, etc.

    Adds from magazines for getting free travel brochures with color photos from other lands (try "Sunset" or "Holiday" Magazines)

    Addresses for free seed catalogs, and other catalogs

    Addresses for free brochures on such things as prefab houses, which will come in handy when children are looking for ideas for "houses" to build in the yard

Government bulletins (send to U.S. Government Printing Office, Washington D.C. for their list of pamphlets on every subject conceivable.)

United Nations materials, address to: United Nations, New York, New York

You'll find this file growing once you establish a place for it in your school. Involve the children in collecting more stuff for it. Remember, it's lots of fun getting things in the mail.

e. A "ballot box" by the door labeled "We're collecting trading stamps to get equipment for the school. Save your stamps for us."

f. Lockers for children's personals, made of discarded orange crates, milk-man's boxes, or secondhand lumber

g. Type up a list of things you need with prices noted clearly. Hang this up in a place conspicuous to parents, teachers, and visitors. Letter a sign to go above it:

BUY US A GIFT
We need the following
things for our school.

Give people a chance to give.

HIGH SCHOOL WORK SPACES

Because of the nature of the high school program (see page 46) work spaces will be determined by the students, and should grow from their suggestions. For that reason, a list of possible work spaces and materials is not included here.

FOR FURTHER SUGGESTIONS

I adapted some of these ideas to my own "Minimal School One." See page 108. For further suggestions on how to set up a classroom, largely from scrap materials, get a copy of "Farralones Scrapbook." (see page 63) It's excellent, and should be a part of every teacher's library.

CURRICULUM

Don't plan a curriculum. When you sit down and work out a plan for what's going to happen, your ego gets involved. Then when the kids don't follow the plan, you get frustrated and angry with them. And learning becomes a drag.

Instead of planning a curriculum, set your energy toward creating a relaxed environment:

• Non authoritarian, non-teacher-centered, child-centered classroom

- Minimal expectations of children
  - a. they don't have to sit in chairs but can move freely from work space to work space
  - b. there are no tests, nor is one child's achievements ever compared with others (i.e., "Johnny is the second best reader in the school.")
  - c. boundaries of action are clearly defined to the children (see page 97)
  - d. time schedules are cut to an absolute minimum
- Provide kids with good stuff to work with.

The teacher's job, then, is:

- Stay out of the children's way (very difficult)
- Define the boundaries of action. (see page 44)
- Keep the classroom shelves stocked with new and interesting stuff. But don't get the idea that it's easy. This kind of teaching is much more difficult than being an authoritarian.

SCHOOL IN A SUITCASE

Here's a way to keep your school stuff together and portable. Great for "treking" schools, minimum schools, and "underground" schools — wherever portability is an asset. Here's what to do:

Get a small footlocker, or large suitcase from your local secondhand store or flea market. Line it with colorful cloth. Glue the cloth to the inside panels with wallpaper paste mixed with a small amount of white glue (about ½ part white glue to 3½ parts wallpaper paste.)

Get six adult-size shoe boxes. You can buy plastic ones, or get cardboard ones free and line and cover them with cloth. Label the boxes to correspond with "School Tools" outlined below.

Here is a list of School Tools.

- PENCILS, AND OTHER STUFF
  - a. pocket watch that works
  - b. a dozen lead pencils
  - c. color crayons
  - d. folding ruler
  - e. water color set
  - f. paint brushes at least ¼ inch wide
  - g. scissors
- READING
  - a. set of small plastic letters, lower and upper case, plus numbers
  - b. 5 x 7 index cards to make your own flashcards (one word to a card)
- MATH
  - a. small abacus with instructions
  - b. set of dominoes
  - c. dice
  - d. flash cards: add, subtract, multiply, divide

e. small plastic triangle, square, circle, rectangle (cut from bottom of old soft plastic dishpan or wastebasket)
- SCIENCE
  a. magnifying glass
  b. magnets and bits of conducting and non-conducting metals
  c. set of small ropes and pulleys
  d. small microscope set
  e. set of transparent plastic "windows" in primary colors (available at good toy stores)
  f. lantern battery, flashlight bulb, and 25 feet of bell wire
- FITS TOGETHER
  a. jigsaw puzzles that child can do
  b. old take-apart clock
  c. variety of small things to take apart
  d. screwdriver and pliers
- COLLECTION BOX
  an empty box for child's own collection of stuff picked up along the way
- YOU'LL ALSO NEED
  a. lined, colored and plain paper (different sizes)
  b. accordian style file folder to hold the paper (get one with an elastic band to hold it closed)
  c. two clipboards (these are the "desks")
  d. variety of books
  - story books
  - world atlas
  - work books for Math, and Spelling
  - coloring books
  e. empty plastic egg carton to teach dozens

With everything stored neatly in the footlocker, school can be set up in a matter of seconds. The tools it contains will provide student and teacher with ready ways and means for learning.

If you want a school in a suitcase made up for you, either to the above specifications or your own, write to:

Reynaldo Cortez
6015 Monterey Avenue
Richmond, CA. 94805

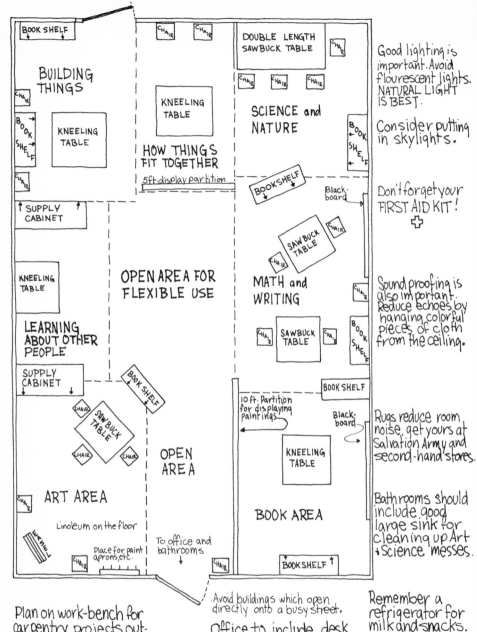

Good lighting is important. Avoid flourescent lights. NATURAL LIGHT IS BEST.

Consider putting in skylights.

Don't forget your FIRST AID KIT! ✛

Sound proofing is also important. Reduce echoes by hanging colorful pieces of cloth from the ceiling.

Rugs reduce room noise, get yours at Salvation Army and second-hand stores.

Bathrooms should include good large sink for cleaning up Art & Science messes.

Remember a refrigerator for milk and snacks.

Plan on work-bench for carpentry projects outside main classroom

Outside Equipment · SWINGS · OLD TIRES · PLAYHOUSE · OLD BOAT · OLD CAR BODY · ETC.

Avoid buildings which open directly onto a busy street.

Office to include desk, filing cabinet, phone and office supplies.

NOTE:
There are no interior walls in the classroom — except display partitions. BROKEN LINES DESIGNATE WORK SPACE ONLY.

Linda Bennett

6

WHAT WE DO ALL DAY LONG

WHAT TO LOOK FOR IN A SCHOOL

The section below entitled "A Day In The Life Of" describes a small school in a church. On the day I observed and wrote the description, there were twenty-three children present. They ranged in ages from five to twelve.

While reading the description, notice the following points in particular:

- The teacher's role in the program is minimal. None of the activities appear to center on her. She is a participant; she does not direct.
- The children move freely from one activity to another. They are free to choose what they want to do — instead of having the teacher make choices for them.
- The children learn through exploration and discovery, communicating their discoveries to others around them through words and actions. They learn by *doing*, instead of reading about other people doing in books.
- The teacher intrudes in the children's affairs only once. This is when Peter comes to her in need of adult assurance, and the teacher recognizes this and gives it freely. But notice, too, how she turns the responsibility back to the children when she tells Chris to talk to Peter, not her.

This is just one program in operation. It will guide you toward the kind of free curriculum I work with and many people are exploring. For further experience with the open classroom concept, visit a free school near you.

A DAY IN THE LIFE OF

Upon entering the classroom at 9:30, the adult's impression is one of noisy chaos. But the children's spontaneous movements and openness indicate that they are comfortable in this environment and probably don't see it as chaotic at all.

The following is a list of activities which take place in the course of such a day: evidence of productivity in the midst of what might otherwise pass for purposelessness.

9:30 Art
The teacher, Pat, straightens up the art table from the activities of the day before.
John, who is ten, mixes up new paint for the painting easel.

9:30 Resting
Niki and Brian, who are six years old each, lounge in the book corner. Brian is lying back on a large pillow, nearly asleep.

9:30 Reading
Niki sits beside Brian. She is reading a book to herself.

10:00 Nature
Hanna, the volunteer, has taken five children on a nature walk along nearby roads and trails.

10:00 Math
Pat sits at a table with four children. They are working on a Math lesson. Only two children have books. They are telling Pat how many disks to flip over on the abacus — which is part of their exercises. The two children with books know how to do Math. The other two kids are watching so that they can learn, too.

10:15 Playing house
Jenny, who is five years old, is playing with Paul and Barbara in the backyard playhouse. Paul and Barbara are seven years old. They play the roles of the mother and father, while Jenny plays the role of the child.
(Through role playing, children test new ways to relate to their peers, and thus to the world. The learning here is important, though it is non-academic.)

10:25 Math
At the game table inside, three children are playing dominoes. Games like dominoes, checkers, and any game using dice, provide a stimulus for learning numbers, and provide the children with practical application of their knowledge.

10:40 Reading
Pat sits down on the big lounging pillows scattered in the book corner. Several children leave other activities to join her there. They pick out books and bring them for her to read to them.

11:00 More Reading

Pat has read one story to the children. Then Alice, age nine, wants to read aloud to the others. Pat turns over the reading to her.

11:15 Art

By eleven o'clock, there are several new paintings hanging on the drying rack near the easel.

Susan, age seven, is taking down paintings from the day before and is putting new ones on the display panels which are fastened along one entire wall.

11:15 How things fit together

Two children are working together on a jigsaw puzzle. They have been working on it for nearly an hour. It is about half done.

11:20 Making maps

One child is tracing maps from a large world Atlas.

11:25 Building houses

Three boys, Michael, Sean, and Peter are in the back yard building a house with panels cut from heavy cardboard. They are fastening the panels together with pipe cleaners looped through holes punched in the cardboard.

11:30 Other countries

Noel, age 11, is off by herself in a quiet corner. She is writing a story about a girl growing up in India. She has already studied about life in India from a book. Her story is for a book that she and Barbara are making together. Pat makes mimeographed copies of the children's stories, and the children staple them together like books.

11:30 Making books

There are more than a dozen books made by children at the school. Some are about Math, others about Writing, or Geography, or History. There is one book about repairing bicycles, and another about a trip to Mars.

11:40 Fighting

Peter runs into the room from the playground. He is screaming and holding the back of his head. He runs to Pat and tells her that Chris hit him with a stick. Pat looks at Peter's head and finds a small bump, assuring him in the process that he is okay. The injury is not serious.

11:45 Using language

Pat tells Peter to go back to the playground and ask Chris to come inside. Moments later, Chris comes into the room shouting: "He was pulling out the pipe cleaners. He . . ." Pat cuts him short. "Don't tell me about it," she says. "Tell Peter."

Chris turns to Peter. They begin to yell at each other. But it doesn't explode into a fight. Their voices become calmer, and in less than three minutes they are back outside playing together.

12:00 Eating, sharing, and making plans

At noon, Hanna returns with five children from the nature walk. And then it's time for lunch. The tables are cleared of the mornings activities, and the children sit down to eat their lunches, brought from home. Much talking, trading food back and forth, with Pat on the telephone during most of it and Hanna talking about starting a sprouter to grow alfalfa sprouts.

1:00 Libraries and gardens

After lunch, Pat picks five children to go with her to the library. There are hassles, and tears in the process, since someone who wants to go is always, it seems, being left behind.

Hanna resolves the problem when she asks for volunteers to work with her in the vegetable garden which she has started behind the school.

Later in the day

School is out at 2:00. Some parents come to pick up their children in cars. A few children walk home. But at 3:30 everyone has not yet left. There are projects going on which cannot, it appears, be interrupted. At 4:00 Pat tells everyone to go home. It is nearly 4:30 by the time she locks up.

PLANS AND SCHEDULES

In this school there are no lesson plans. The teacher seldom prepares special projects. There are no time schedules, and no homework. There are no right or wrong answers. If a time schedule exists, it follows the seemingly unstructured drift of the child's own interests, moving from Math, to Reading, to playing outside, and back to Math, sometimes all in the space of an hour.

WORK SPACES

The teachers part in all this is to set up work spaces and then to allow the children to explore these spaces freely. The teacher keeps the work spaces well stocked and in good condition, making them appealing and interesting to the children by keeping an eye out for new things to add to them from time to time.

ACTION BOUNDARIES

Whatever structure exists in the classroom will apply toward discovering, defining, and enforcing the boundaries of action. *Example:* The teacher makes it clear that books cannot be thrown. This action boundary is stated simply and directly: "The rule is that you can't throw books. If you break this rule, you will have to leave the book space and play somewhere else." It is stated that way to the children.

Each rule comprises a contract between the child and the teacher, and between the child and other children. For the child, the logic goes like this: "The rule is that no kids can throw books. I won't throw books because when I do I have to leave the book space. The teacher or one of the other kids will make me leave. I feel fairly safe from being hit by books then. Hardly anyone throws them because hardly anyone wants to have to leave the book space." This system is not infallible, any more than stop signs and speed limit signs on our highways are infallible. It only offers enough order to the world to make life manageable.

Everyone has limits. Some people can't tolerate loud noises. Others feel best when surrounded by activity and noise. The Ten Commandments can be viewed as Moses' understanding of universal human action boundaries. In a school, it is important to discover the boundaries which work best for everyone, and then to create an effective means of dealing with them.

CHILDREN LEARN BY DOING

The classroom described above is a place where people — children as well as adults — learn by *doing*. The principle is quite simple if you compare the process of learning how to read, or write, or do anything, to learning how to ride a bicycle. You can learn what a bicycle looks like from a book. Your intellect can even grasp the concept of balancing, turning, pedaling, and stopping from a book. But you have not learned how to ride a bike until you have actually gotten on and then, after much practice and many falls, have ridden off by yourself.

Example: Children learn how to read by recognizing letters on a page, and then seeing how letters become words, and words become sentences that communicate ideas and/or images. They do all this by seeing the writing on the page, and figuring out what it all means. A seven year old boy explained it this way:

> "I learned how to read by sounding out letters. You should
> learn how to read by real easy books. And you keep on
> going and going, and when you think it's time to have real
> hard books, you should have them."

If you distrust this simplicity, reflect on the fact that your students have already learned how to talk, and they did not do this by being told where to put their tongue and lips and how to vibrate the sound box in their throats. They learned it by doing it. They did it by exploring sounds, by feeling the way their tongues, mouths, and sound boxes felt when they made different noises. Educators agree that learning to speak is far more complex than learning how to read and write, and in most cases children will learn to read on their own if they are placed in an environment where books are accessible and where reading is highly valued.

TEACHERS LEARN BY DOING

By the same token, adults who want to teach in the kind of school setting described here will learn how to do it by doing it. There is a point beyond which books can be of no use. Once the classroom is set up (see page 33), and the basic principles of setting action boundaries are understood (see pages 44 and 97), you will learn how to handle the classroom simply by being there day after day. It will be much like learning how to ride a bicycle; after much practice, and many falls, you'll learn how to do it. Remember, there are no such things as right and wrong answers in such a setting — not even for the teacher.

HOW YOU MAKE IT WORK

It will take patience and time to establish this kind of "freedom." Freedom is an extremely vague term: freedom to what? Burn down the school? Obviously not. There are limits, so you might as well make them clear from the start.

And there'll be the problem of deciding how much "formalized" study, if any, is to be established. You'll find, though, that just having the work spaces well set up will be stimulus enough for most children. After a few months, you'll gain confidence in the children who are doing okay on their own, and will be able to leave them to their own devices while you turn your attention to those less motivated.

Teachers must liberate themselves from the concept of "school," and must relinquish the traditional role as *master*. They'll probably have to work at gaining respect for the child's own capacity to explore, discover, and learn.

Focus on the child, and respect him at all times. His autonomy will grow in direct proportion to how much responsibility the teacher allows him to exercise in the processes of making his own choices, standing up for himself, and trying out new things.

DOING IT IN HIGH SCHOOL

The high schools I visited followed the same general direction as the school described above, with the exception of these important differences:
- The process of defining, setting, and enforcing action boundaries is carried out by the students, although teachers do insist that it be done, through:
    a. Daily "grief sessions" run by the students, in which the workability of old and new rules is discussed, and violators are questioned.
    b. Teachers assume the same status in grief sessions as students
- Educational focus is on the practical application of skills being learned. This is made possible by the pressence of:

a. pottery wheel and kiln
b. large architect's model of a city (made by the students from cardboard and wood, and used for "urban planning" projects.)
c. jewelry-making table and tools
d. auto repair shop
e. bi-monthly magazine published by students, using mimeo machine
f. small electronic computer purchased and constructed by students from a kit
g. small portable stage for theater, with public performances occasionally held in the parks.
h. students volunteering time and labor to community action projects outside the school (Other schools, Head Start, Redevelopment Agency, Legal Aid, Tutorial Programs, County Schools Special Education for Hard of Hearing, etc.)
i. space for rehearsal of student rock band (evenings)
j. studio space for painters and sculptors
k. regularly scheduled classes in Literature, Driver's Training, History, Political Science, Letter Writing, Poetry Writing, Filling out Government Forms, Test-Taking Skills, Exploring Laymen's Resources In Law, Filmmaking, High School Equivalency Coaching, Birth Control (Many of these classes can be held in the evening, led by people working in the field they are teaching.)

- Attendance is voluntary

HIGH SCHOOL APPRENTICESHIP

Here's some people who are into setting up apprenticeships for high school students — anywhere in the U.S. and Canada, as I understand it. They put students in touch with teachers, and set it up so that you get high school credit. Write to them for more information:

Apprenticeship Service Program
P.O. Box 908
Montara, California 94037

It could very well fit into your plans.

ALTERNATIVE COLLEGES AND UNIVERSITIES

The number of free universities across the nation is growing. They offer the structure to put together any course you might want to teach or learn. If there's a free university near you, you'll be able to find it through your local underground press.

Goddard College in Plainfield, Vermont, offers a Master's Degree without taking courses, and without going to Plainfield. The M.A. is granted on the basis of a project which the student wants to do. For more information on this, write:

GRADUATE PROGRAM OFFICE
Goddard College
Plainfield, Vermont 05667

For still more information on higher education, including high school, read *The Soft Revolution,* by Postman and Weingartner, Delta $1.95.

BOOKLIST

1. *Teacher,* Sylvia Ashton-Warner, Bantam $1.25
2. *A Child's Mind,* Muriel Beadle, DD Anchor $2.95
3. *The School That I'd Like,* edited by Edward Blishen, Penguin $ .95
4. *The Art of Teaching,* Gilbert Highet, Vintage $1.95
5. *How Children Learn,* John Holt, Dell $ .95
6. *The Open Classroom,* Herbert Kohl, Vintage $1.65
7. *A Parent's Guide to Children's Reading,* Nancy Larrick, Pocket Books $ .95
8. *Freedom, Not License,* A. S. Neill, Hart $1.95
9. *The Language And Thought of the Child,* Jean Piaget, Meridian $2.95
10. *Children and Science,* Lazer Goldberg, Scribners $2.95

7

PLANS FOR BUILDING
YOUR OWN EQUIPMENT

PRIMARY SCHOOL FURNITURE

The plans in this section are for constructing primary school equipment, which because of its size is otherwise difficult to buy. Some schools have experimented with cutting down adult-sized furniture bought at secondhand stores; tables work out okay, but large chair seats are not comfortable for younger children, even after you've cut down the legs.

The furniture in the following pages was designed to be constructed with simple hand tools, by people with only minimum carpentry skills. At the same time, the furniture is strong and practical.

Here's a list of tools you'll need:
- Hammer
- Crosscut saw
- Pliers or crescent wrench
- Coping saw, or electric saber saw
- Hand drill or electric drill
- ¼ inch drill bit

When you've put together your furniture have the kids help sand and finish it. Proper finishing, with varnish or high gloss enamel, will prevent slivers and add color to the room.

Furniture for older children — twelve and up — can, of course be adult-sized. You can buy chairs and tables at secondhand stores, and garage sales for less than it'd cost to construct them from scratch. Any other equipment can be designed and built by the students.

KNEELING TABLE

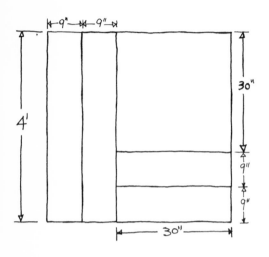

Use one 4' x 4' panel of ¾" plywood and one 5 ft. length of 2"x 4".

That's all you'll need if you cut it right. So do it this way.

You'll also need white glue and #4 by 3 inch nails.

Cut the 2"x 4" into four 14 inch lengths - these are the legs.

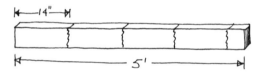

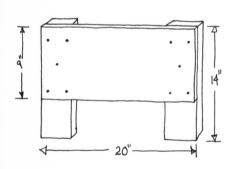

Fasten a 20" length of 9 inch plywood to the legs. Make two of these.

Note: Put chrome coasters on bottoms of legs to save floors later on.

Remember: Glue all joints!

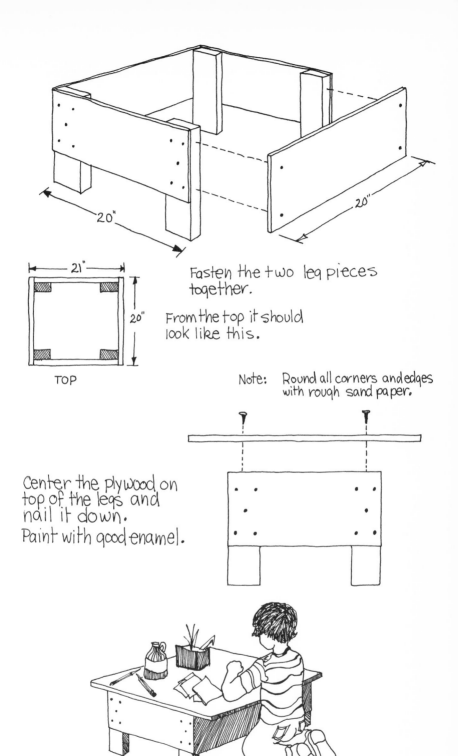

21"

20"

20"

20"

TOP

Fasten the two leg pieces together.

From the top it should look like this.

Note: Round all corners and edges with rough sand paper.

Center the plywood on top of the legs and nail it down.
Paint with good enamel.

CHAIR

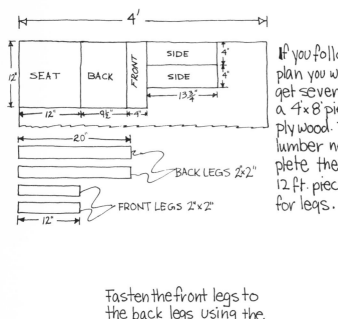

If you follow this cutting plan you will be able to get seven chairs out of a 4'x8' piece of half-inch plywood. The only other lumber needed to complete them will be four 12 ft. pieces of 2x2 fir for legs.

Fasten the front legs to the back legs using the plywood side.
Make two of these.

Use white glue and nails.

Fasten front piece to legs.

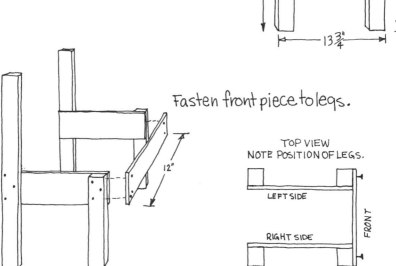

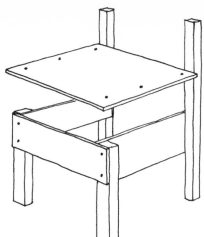

Glue and nail the seat.

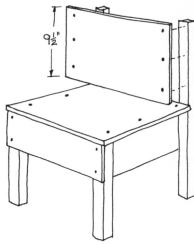

$9\frac{1}{2}$"

Glue and nail the back.

Sand the edges and corners. Paint with good enamel.

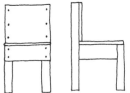

FRONT VIEW   SIDE VIEW

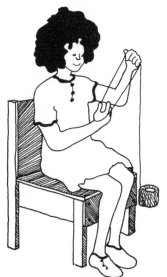

EQUIPMENT SHELF

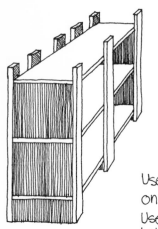

This is a very sturdy equipment shelf.

Get some 1"x12" pine or fir. Cut four 10" pieces for the sides. Use three 30" pieces as the shelves.

Use eight 1"x3" stringers on front and back. Use 2"x4"'s on the bottom.

|← 11¾" →|

10"

Cut sides like this

These drawings will show how the pieces go together.

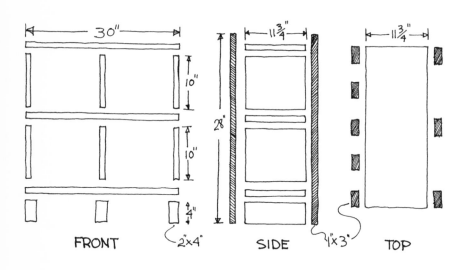

30"

10"

10"

28"

¾"

FRONT   2"x4"   11¾"   SIDE   1"x3"   11¾"   TOP

SAWBUCK TABLE

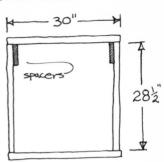

Build a frame 30" square out of 1"x 3"s - use glue and nails. Add some 1"x3" spacers to one end. These are for the legs.

Place a piece of half inch plywood 30" square over the top of the frame. That is the top of the table.

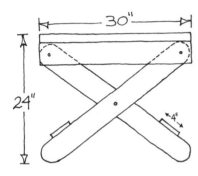

Cut four 1"x 4"s to 35½". Round the ends. (This way you will not have to calculate any angles.)

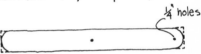

Drill ¼" holes and fasten with ¼" carriage bolts.

Use a 1"x 4" as a cross brace at the bottom.

EASEL

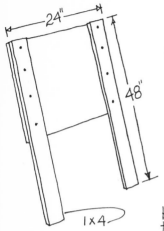

24"

48"

1x4

Use fir or pine 1x4's as legs.
Fasten to edge of ½ inch
ply wood face.

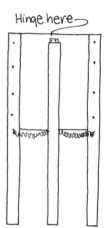

Hinge here

Hinge, using small bolts
to fasten hinge. Use
lightweight chain
fastened with screw-
eyes.

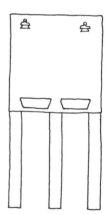

Use large spring clips
to hold paper. 5x9
bread pans to hold
jars of paint. Drill holes
near upper lip of pan
then fasten with wing-
nuts & bolts for easy
removal and cleaning.

Paint easel with high
gloss enamel for
easy cleaning.

TOOLS

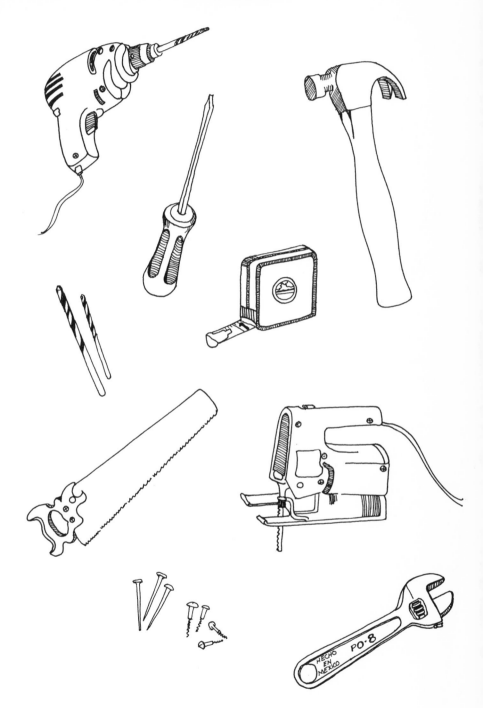

8

SCROUNGING

A LIST OF COMMON MATERIALS

Before buying anything for the classroom, explore the use of discarded materials which can be turned to good use in the school. The resources are broad. Consider the following, which are the most commonly used classroom recylables:

- Egg Cartons
    a. great for collage materials, once the shapes are cut up
    b. two egg cup shapes cut out and glued mouth to mouth, become the head for a finger puppet
    c. the sturdy "styro" cartons are great for storing beads, paper clips, and other small items, and also
    d. for poster paint "pallets" to take to the tables, and also
    e. as candle molds, with parafin and old crayon stubs melted down for wax, and also
    f. with fake eggs (see page 34) for the Math work space
- Old Magazines
    a. kids like them better than anything else for making collages
    b. cut out pictures and paste on cardboard for visual social studies kit (see page 36)
- Tin Cans
    a. use for mixing poster paint and leave them at the easel
    b. coffee cans with sealing plastic lids are almost indispensable for storing pencils, crayons, etc.

- Last Years Calendars

    For the Math work space, cut squares from 1 x 3 pine, sand, cut out large calendar numbers and glue on pine blocks, finish overall with Varathane for long lasting, good looking surface
- Old Tires

    a. Great, of course, for a playground swing

    b. Or just stack up a dozen and let the kids go to work on them

    c. *"Farrallones Scrapbook"* people have worked out lots more uses for tires. (See Booklist page 63)
- Broken Clocks, and Other Small Machinery

    give the kids a screwdriver and pliers and let them find out what's inside – how things work
- Paper Sacks

    when you can't get paper elsewhere, cut the large grocery store sacks into 10 x 10 inch squares, or larger, choosing the least wrinkled surfaces to cut from. The kids like this paper, and it's fine for crayon drawing, painting, and just plain old writing
- Mason Jars, Peanut Butter Jars, Jam Jars

    For the science work space – collecting bugs, worms, etc.
- Plastic Quart Bleach Bottles

    Collect several, then cut to the right size, using a measuring cup, for ½ cup, one cup, two cup, three cup, and four cup graduated measuring set for the Math area.
- Large Television Set

    Take out the innards, and let the kids turn the old case into a hand puppet theater.
- Supply Sources for Wood

    a. Seashores and riverbanks

    b. cabinetmaker's scrap box

    c. lumber supply company scrap box

    d. orange crates

    e. wrecking yard
- Old Cars are Good

    An old car parked on the playground is a child's dream come true. One school that I visited had an ancient fire engine, a defunct caterpillar tractor, and a broken down motorcycle, donated to them over a period of nearly ten years. Another school had a big old rotten-hulled boat.
- Cardboard

    See *Farralones Scrapbook.* They're the experts on this.
- Cable Spools

    Don't forget about those big spools that hold telephone and electric wire when you're looking for tables for the classroom. They're not easy for private citizens to get, but the utility companies are more generous to schools. Get hold of someone in the maintenance yard and ask them to save you some.

- Plastic Scraps

  Coffee can lids, made of pliable plastic, are fine for cutting out geometric shapes for the Math corner. Collect different colors, and cut out shapes with scissors. Plastic letters and numbers can be cut from the lids, too, using a dime store letter stencil, and a matt knife. Thicker shapes and figures can be cut from old plastic dish pans and wastebaskets. How about making picture-less, reversible, plastic jigsaw puzzles?

- Telephone System

  Did you know that the big phone companies give old model phones to schools, to be hooked up with a six volt drycell battery for a real, functioning phone system for the kids? Call their public relations department for information about this.

- Paper

  My publisher says: "Don't get hung up in an 8½ x 11 inch world. Printers and paper companies get left with weird-sized paper cut from larger pieces on special jobs." Some places give it away, others sell it at a fraction of the cost of standard-sized paper. The sources are:
  - newspaper printing plants
  - industrial printers
  - offset printing shops
  - large paper supply houses

  Use the yellow pages of your phone book to locate these people. Look under "Printers" and "Paper: Wholesale and Retail."

- Trading Stamps

  See page 37.

- Free Movies

  Here's a book that lists over 5,000 good films to use in the classroom, mostly stuff like travelogs and documentaries. Get the catalog from:

  > Educators Progress Service, Inc.
  > Randolph, Wisconsin 53956

  The catalog is called "Educator's Guide to Free Films," and it costs around $15. That may sound like a lot of money, until you start looking into how much it costs to rent a film.

- Junk Mail

  Bring those fat, unopened envelopes to school and put them in a classroom mailbox. Younger kids enjoy "opening mail" and sometimes they find neat stuff inside, like pictures, coupons, and some of the strangest graphic art work in the world. Once in a while you get some good nature photos, too, like from those "Life Magazine" Science Series ads.

- Your Head

I'm sure you can come up with a hundred more ideas, but this will get you started. Once you do venture out on this trail, you'll see how much trash we generate in our lives, and how much of it is reusable. But don't collect junk for the sake of seeing how much you can accumulate. Take it to school only when you have a specific use for it.

BUYING MATERIALS

There are some things you probably won't be able to scrounge, like pencils, crayons, and books. Here are four possibilities for buying them economically:

- Buy your materials through government surplus at a fraction of the retail cost (see page 62).
- Line up a sympathetic merchant who'll sell to you wholesale.
- Have each parent buy $5 to $10 worth of materials every few months, thus reducing the burden on any one person. Do this by making up a list, with prices, and having each parent go out and buy his portion of the things that the school needs.
- Charge each parent a materials fee of so much per year. This will create a materials budget to work from.

Most wholesalers of educational materials will sell to small schools but don't ordinarily give much of a discount over retail prices until you're ordering in quantities like for three to four hundred students. My experience has been that local merchants are more generous than the big wholesalers, once you discuss your needs with them. If you do want to contact a wholesaler, they are listed in your phone book under "School Supplies."

ECHOES FROM THE WHOLE EARTH PEOPLE

The Last Whole Earth Catalog — something every school should have — lists the following free catalogs.

For *Instructional Aids, Materials, Supplies*

- Follow Through Project
  Educational Development Center
  55 Chapel Street
  Newton, Mass. 02160

For *Playground Equipment*

- Council for Parks and Playgrounds
  15 Gramercy Park
  New York, New York 10003

For *Music, and Dance Equipment*

- Children's Music Center, Inc.
  5373 West Pico Blvd.
  Los Angeles, California 90019

Drop any of these people a postcard, and say, "Please send me your free catalog of (whatever it is)." Don't forget to include your return address.

GOVERNMENT SURPLUS

Once you've established yourself as a non-profit corporation, (see page 76) you will be eligible to receive government surplus. Remember, this means everything from paper clips to land in the country. Surplus property is available from both Federal and State governments, and policy varies on getting it.

To contact the right people at the Federal level, telephone the U.S. Government "Information" number (see your phone book) in the city nearest you, and ask them how to contact the "Surplus Property Branch." Then call or write that office and ask how your organization can buy government surplus.

In California, State surplus is handled by the "State Educational Agency for Surplus Property," and most States will have some counterpart of this office located at the State Capitol. Telephone "Information" for your State Capitol (telephone company "Information" is free even if you're calling from the next State — just dial the proper area code, then 555-1212), and ask for a listing for the State Surplus Property Officer. Then contact that office by phone or mail and ask them to tell you about the steps for getting surplus property. In California:

> State Educational Agency for Surplus Property
> 721 Capitol Mall
> Sacramento, California 95814

BOOKLIST

1. *American Boys Handy Book,* D.C. Beard, from Tuttle Co., Inc., Rutland, Vermont 05701 $3.95
2. *Farrallones Scrapbook*, Farrallones Designs, Star Route, Point Reyes, California $4.00
3. *The Great International Airplane Book*, Mander, Dippel, and Gossage, Simon & Shuster $2.95
4. *Simple Working Models of Historic Machines*, Aubrey F. Burnstal, M.I.T. Press, 50 Ames St., Cambridge, Mass. $3.95
5. *The Last Whole Earth Catalog*, Random House $5.00
6. *Educator's Guide To Free Films*, Educator's Progress Service, Randolph, Wisconsin 53596 $10.75
7. *700 Science Experiments For Everyone*, Doubleday $4.50
8. *Push Back The Desks*, Albert Cullum, Four Winds Press $2.50
9. *Catalog of Free Teaching Materials*, Gordon Salisburg, P.O. Box 1075, Ventura, California $2.68
10. *The Workshop for Learning Things Catalog*, 5 Bridgeport Street, Watertown, Mass. 02172 $.50

9

WHO'S MINDING THE STORE?

COMPLAINTS DEPARTMENT

One of the greatest failures of small schools, as well as small businesses, is that no one pays attention to the business routines. No one answers the phone. No one opens the mail. No one knows who talks to parents. No one pays the bills. No one keeps the records. No one signs the checks. No one keeps appointments. Like, EVERYBODY'S OUT TO LUNCH.

If you can present some semblance of order in the day to day business of operating a school, you'll minimize the problem of alienating the community.

NEIGHBORS

One of the first things a small school discovers is this: the neighbors. Neighbors call the law when they see kids on the roof. Neighbors complain to the health department when they see the garbage cans flowing over. Neighbors call the school to donate a used swing set only to find that the phone has been disconnected. Neighbors drop by to see about getting their kids into your school and no one will talk to them. Neighbors call the local Superintendent of Schools to report that a couple of your kids have wandered down to the grocery store for penny candy.

Unless you acknowledge your neighbors, and learn how to deal with them effectively, you're going to be in for some unpleasant surprises. The curious ones, who might have been your supporters, become indifferent. The indifferent ones become hostile. And the hostile ones declare war.

But all this happens without your knowing it; because you've been ignoring the neighbors, you can't possibly know what's going on in their heads. Then suddenly everyone is rousting you: the education department, the little old lady next door, the health department, the fire department, and City Hall. And you're screaming "persecution," and the paranoia level of the school has gone up a hundred points. How to avoid all the nonsense is called "Minding the Store."

DAMNED DAILY ROUTINES

Dividing up the chores is the first step toward getting it together. It is somebody's job to develop a sense of the overall operation, and figure out ways to get others to help keep the place in shape. How do you get others to help? (see page 81)

Figuring out what needs to be done isn't as easy as it appears. To help with this, I've compiled the following list:

- Petty Tasks
    a. Carry out the trash
    b. Sweep the floor
    c. Clean up the yard
    d. Repair broken windows, toilets, toys, furniture
    e. Exterminate varmints
- General Office
    a. Buy stamps, envelopes, misc.
    b. Open mail
    c. Answer the phone
    d. Keep files in order
        Emergency information
        Attendance records
        Student files
    e. Answer correspondence — the most time consuming of all
- Heavy Routines
    a. Pay the bills
    b. Collect tuitions
    c. Daily bookkeeping, monthly, quarterly and yearly accounting
    d. File Income Tax (quarterly and annually)
    e. Write checks
    f. Interview (see page 87)
        New students
        Parents
        New teachers

g. Talk to the insurance man (most irritating)

h. Deal with personnel problems (most time consuming)

i. Keep the authorities content

j. Publicity (Making and mailing brochures, holding public events, etc.)

KEEPING THE RECORDS STRAIGHT

If you get into paying rent, paying people, buying materials, and collecting tuition fees, you will need to keep records. Bookkeeping and general office routines can be kept at a minimum with the right tools. Some people do it from their checkbook, and on the backs of envelopes. But that system has its limits, especially if you ever wanted to turn the job over to someone else. After rapping with people in small businesses and schools, I got together a list of workable tools for the front office. Here's that list, with current prices:

1- "Dome Simplified Weekly Bookkeeping Record*
   Order Number 600, retail price $4.50

2- "Dome Payroll Book, 1—25 Employees"*
   Order number 625, retail price $3.50

The next three items come from *Rediform, Inc.,* and are standard items that you should have no difficulty finding.

3- "Weekly Time Ticket"
   Order number 4K409, retail price $1.00 for 300

4- "Statements"
   Order number 8K884, retail price 75¢ per 100

5- "Money Receipt Book"
   Order number 8K826, retail price $1.68 per 300

You should also get:

6- "Tops, 'Avoid Verbal Orders'"
   Order number 3373, retail price 45¢ per 300

Although not on the list, you'll need a commercial checking account. When shopping around for a bank, be sure to ask if they can handle "Federal Tax Deposits." If they can't, go somewhere that can. You'll discover why on page 136.

There's no need for me to go into detail on items 1 and 2 because they contain their own excellent and simple directions. They are designed to be used by non-bookkeepers, meaning you and me, brother. The payroll book

---

* Dome Publishing, Inc.
   Dome Building
   Providence, R.I. 02903

contains tables for Federal Withholding and Social Security deductions. The bookkeeping record contains printed columns for deductible expenses. They're tremendously useful tools.

Item 3, "Weekly Time Ticket," is something you'll need only if you're paying people by the hour. It's where they record their time — time cards, in short.

Item 4, "Statements," are what you send to parents when their tuition fees are due.

Item 5, "Money Receipts," are what you give parents after they've paid.

Item 6, "Avoid Verbal Orders," are what you put by the phone to record telephone messages.

Total cost of the front office package: $11.88 plus tax (fall 1971.)

Other items you'll eventually need will be:

a telephone directory in which to record your own numbers,

a rubber stamp with your school's name and address,

a typewriter with elite typeface,

stamps, pencils, paper, envelopes, erasers, a desk.

How much you spend on all that will depend on your scrounging ability (see page 58) and your budget, so I'll leave all that up to you.

WHAT YOU SHOULD HAVE IN YOUR FILES

You can buy a hand-carried, metal, fire-proof file box, of the type made for home use, for around $4.50. A couple more dollars will buy you a year's supply of file folders. A minimum file should contain:

- File A: Official Documents
    a. A copy of your "Private School Affidavit" (see page 114)
    b. A list of courses offered (see page 15)
    c. Names, addresses, and educational backgrounds of each faculty member
    d. Enrollment list of students presently enrolled
    e. Any licenses required by city/county
- File B: Student Records (a separate file folder for each student)
    a. Family information: names, addresses, etc.
    b. List of courses the student has completed
    c. Any correspondence regarding student
- File C: Health Department Stuff
    Health reports from physician on each student (See page 116)
- File D: Emergency Procedures
    This would include numbers to call and what to do in the event of fire, accident, earthquake and other natural disasters. Include a First Aid Manual, available from most book stores for a dollar.

In addition to the above, you should have,

- File E: Emergency Information

    Make 4 x 5 cards with Emergency Information for each student (see page 00.) Keep them in an appropriate file box, one of those little metal ones you get at the dime store for 59¢. This file box, with cards filled out, should be kept in the classroom or close to the telephone. For the proper form to follow, see page 115.

    File E will be indispensable when Johnny falls off the roof and breaks his arm, or when Jimmy goes into convulsions. Instruct each staff member on the use of these cards in the event of emergency. It may just save your school a serious lawsuit or two.

FIGURE OUT HOW MUCH TUITION TO CHARGE

Unfortunately, money or the lack of it may determine if your school succeeds or fails. Unless you have a wealthy patron, you'll have to charge tuition. Here's how to figure out how much to charge:

- Put together a budget. The following is a model:

Rent	$150 per month
Utilities	75 per month
Insurance	25 per month
Materials	50 per month
Salary	475 per month
Fringe benefits	30 per month
Maintenance	100 per month
Incidentals	30 per month
SUB TOTAL	$835 per month
plus 10% leeway	83 per month
TOTAL	$918 per month

    Get the most accurate figures you can, based on your own operation.
- Take the total number of children enrolled and subtract 10% for fees lost when children drop out and new students aren't immediately enrolled.
    a. 30 students usually enrolled
    b. minus 3 students = 27 students
- Divide the total monthly costs by the number of students:
    $918 ÷ 27 = $34
    Each student would then be charged $34 per month.
- It's a good idea to bank extra capital in the event of a crisis:
    a. if you charge an extra $5 per month, that's a total of $135 per month you'll be able to bank
    b. charge $10 per month extra; bank $270 per month
- Collection of fees is the major pitfall of many small schools. More than one school has gone under because parents wouldn't pay their fees. Two solutions are suggested:

a. have parents pay a full year in advance, refundable if they drop in the middle of the year: $34 monthly is $306 yearly.

b. have parents sign a banknote for the yearly tuition. Then the bank becomes the collector.

- Understand in figuring a budget that most schools operate for nine months only. The building stands unused for three months. Unless you've got an unusual landlord, you still must pay the rent. There are two things you can do about this:

a. run a summer session to meet expenses (no need for a credentialed teacher for that)

b. figure out a budget for a full year, including the cost of maintaining the building during the summer. Divide this figure by the number of students that you ordinarily enroll. That will give the yearly tuition cost per child. To get the monthly figure based on the nine months school year, divide by nine instead of twelve. That's the tuition cost if you're running for only nine months but charging the students to maintain the building for the summer.

INSURANCE

If you're renting a space for a school, you'll have to get into buying insurance. To do this, get hold of a reputable insurance broker. Don't run blind in this; don't simply lift names from the phone book. Instead go around and ask merchants and small business people, who you know, what they do for insurance. Ask them who their insurance brokers are, and keep asking until you get a satisfactory recommendation.

If you really can't find a good agent this way, you'll have to start phoning brokers who are listed in the phone book. Get them to come out, look over your premises, and make bids on your insurance needs. Ask lots of questions. Put the agents in the position of being your teachers. Learn as much as you can about their game; it will take a lot of time, but it's well worth it if you're going to be running a school. You'll be insuring yourself from being ripped off by an unscrupulous agent or broker.

Here's a place to start: If you are renting — say from a Church — assume that none of their insurance covers you. You will then want to ask the insurance broker about buying a "Broad Liability Contract," or a "Comprehensive Liability Contract:" known by different names by different folks. In essence, these are packages which should cover the following:

- *premises liability and property damage:* if one of your kids throws a rock through the stained glass window this will pay for repairs
- *Personal injury on premises:* if the minister's wife comes to visit you, slips on a roller skate and cracks her skull, this will pay to fix her head
- *Fire legal liability:* insures you, and your landlord, for your rented space in the event of fire

- *non-owned auto:* if a volunteer drives through the dime store window while getting pencils for you, you are liable for damages because that person was acting as your agent. This will cover you.

You'll also want to ask about:

- *owned auto liability:* to cover any auto registered in the school's name
- *vandalism insurance:* to cover you if someone breaks in and tears the place up
- *workman's compensation:* this covers injuries to your employees while on the job — and is available from the state in most cases. It's a requirement if you have regular paid employees. (See below for more on this.)
- *volunteer accident insurance coverage:* this covers injuries to your students, and is usually purchased by the parent at less than $10 per year under a group plan with your school.

It sounds like all this would cost a fortune, but don't despair. I talked with several schools about their insurance costs. Although each had pretty much the same packages, their situations varied as to the location of the building, the kind of building, and the number of students and employees involved. Because of this their costs varied too: from $17.50 per month to $38 per month.

WORKMAN'S COMPENSATION INSURANCE

This is a good thing to have, especially if you have more than two employees. Workmen's Compensation Insurance can be purchased either from State or private insurance companies.

Benefits are fairly broad, especially when you consider the cost:

- *Medical* — cover's medical expenses for fixing any work-related injury to the employee
- *Attorney Fees* — covers costs of investigating in regard to claim and any court actions in which Workman's Compensation Insurance carrier is involved
- *Paycheck Insurance* — after employee is out of work for more than seven days as a result of the work-related injury, he can claim for payroll compensation

The cost to the employer is 41¢ per $100 of payroll. In other words, if you pay a person $5,000 annually, your insurance would cost $20.50 annually. The State insurance people require that you deposit an amount based on 41¢ per $100 of prospective payroll with them at the beginning of the year. If your payroll is less than you had foreseen at the end of the year, you would get a refund. If it's more, you'd pay more.

You can apply for this insurance either through a private agent, or through the State. For the State insurance, look up the office nearest you under the State listings in your telephone book.

PAYROLL DEPARTMENT

The Federal Government, Internal Revenue Service, requires that every employer keep records of wages paid to employees, and further that employers withhold Federal taxes from employees' wages and deposit these withholdings in a Federal Reserve account on a quarterly basis. If you're going to get into the payment of wages, write or phone your nearest IRS (telephone book under U.S. Gov't) and ask them to send you "Circular E: Employer's Tax Guide." For my description of how you use this stuff, see page 136, "How to pay wages the right way."

FILING INCOME TAX

I'm not going to deal with filing income tax for the school here. That's a subject for another book. But if your school does get so large that it must file income tax reports, say as a corporation, I strongly advise you to get a CPA, unless someone in your group is especially good with such things. CPA's will do the job for a small school for around $35 to $50, according to several school people who do it every year that way.

A non-profit educational organization is exempt from most taxes in the absense of unrelated business income. A Federal income tax return need not be filed (IR Code 501 (C)(3)) but I.R.S. Form 990-A must be submitted yearly within 4 months and 15 days after the close of each fiscal year. In most states a State Franchise Tax filing is not required, however many states require some form of annual report and the State Franchise Tax Board should be consulted in this regard.* For property tax exemptions some states require that the property be used for scientific purposes. "Scientific" has a liberal meaning and scientific purposes should be stated in the corporation purposes clause of the articles if the organization is incorporated in a state with this requirement. In some states educational purposes is sufficient. Probably all states have no exemptions for State and Local sales and use taxes.

RENTING SPACE FROM A CHURCH

Many churches are facing financial crisis and/or are searching for relevant community involvement. They often have large buildings, and church-school classroom space which is not used during week days. Churches have been helpful to many alternative schools. Here's how to ask them for help.

---

* In California an educational organization is exempt from filing an annual information return (Rev & TC Sec. 237 Old) if the organization maintains a regular faculty and curriculum and normally has a regularly organized body of pupils or students in attendance at the place where its educational activities are regularly carried on.

- Pick out a church
  a. If you don't have a church in mind, go to the Yellow Pages of your telephone directory and look under "Churches" for the addresses of churches in the neighborhood where you'd like to be.
  b. Visit these churches and look for one that appears to have empty space during the week days. Also, look for one with a potential outdoor play area, and that seems to have good vibes.
  c. Telephone the church office, as listed in the telephone book. Most churches, of the kind we're talking about, have part-time secretaries who work mornings only. When you contact the secretary, tell her that you represent a private school which is looking for space to rent for a classroom.
  d. Tell the church secretary that you would like to discuss the possibility of renting space from them with the minister of the church. Ask for an appointment to come in and talk with him in person.
  e. At many churches, you may find that the phone is answered by a parishioner volunteering his or her time. You may find they are elderly people who do not quite understand what you mean by "private" school; or have a vision of "alternative" schools as freaky places; or are protecting their church from "outsiders." Don't be put off by such people since they rarely represent the attitudes of the total congregation. Most churches these days tend to be divided between elderly conservatives and young liberals, with the power in the hands of the latter. Insist on talking to the minister. He will give you the clearest picture of the sentiments of the church toward your venture.
- Write Up a Description Of Your Program
  a. Tell who you are: the names and addresses of your leaders, teachers, and your board of directors if you have one. Use titles in front of these names: Director, Educational Director, Consultant, Teacher, Parent.
  b. Tell how many students will be enrolled, and the age group.
  c. Tell what your program is about, but do it briefly, excluding any heavy details. Here's a model:

  > The (name) School is a non-sectarian, ungraded school for children between the ages of five and twelve. The program will be balanced between academic learning and open personal involvement within the child's peer group. It will be supervised by (number) qualified, salaried teachers, and (number) teacher's aides. We will encourage parent involvement since we believe that a child's success in school is often dependent on the parent's understanding of his achievements.

Keep it simple. Remember, you don't want to debate educational philosophies; you want to rent a place for your school.

d. Describe educational backgrounds of your staff. Here's a model:

> Ronald Jones, our Educational Director, taught for two years in the Evergreen School District, and was a consultant to the Evergreen Experimental Schools Project. He is a graduate of Michigan State College, and holds a credential in Elementary Education. He is married, and has two children of his own, ages 3 and 5.

e. A statement of what you understand will be your responsibilities in relation to the church. Here's a model:

> We understand that we will be sharing your facilities and we will make every effort to co-operate with all groups meeting at the church during our hours of operation. In addition, we will expect to be responsible for any additional costs incurred by the church as a result of our presence, such as utilities, maintenance, repair of any damages as a result of the school operation, and the maintenance of our portion of the building in a manner acceptable to the church.

f. Tell what your means of support will be. Here's a model:

> We are a non-profit organization. The school will be supported by small tuition fees and private donations.

g. A statement of what you are able to pay for rent. Here's a model:

> In addition to the costs of utilities and maintenance for the space we use, we will be able to pay up to $75 per month for rent.

- You'll be in a better position to get co-operation from the church if you are established as a non-profit corporation (see page 76). Churches are non-profit too, and usually won't rent to other organizations unless they're established as non-profit. It has to do with their tax problems — keeping donations to the church tax-deductible. So there's no point in your arguing this point if it comes up.

- Type up the Description and have a dozen or more copies made. (You may need them later, in case you don't make it with the first church you approach.)

- Make the whole thing clean and professional. The decision makers, with whom you'll be dealing, usually like things that way.

- Take six copies of your description with you when you go to see the minister because:

  a. It will simplify your communications with him.

  b. He will want to present the description to his board of directors. They're the people who will make the final decision on whether or not to rent space to you.

- Later, you will probably have to go to their board meeting, rap with the group, and work out a lease. (see page 125 for a sample lease contract.)
- If you meet with too much resistance, don't force the issue. You may be able to sell them on renting the space to you, but once you're in you'll never be able to talk them into loving you. Go easy but be open and honest with them. It'll save impossible hassles that might come up after you get the school going.

RENTING A HOUSE

- If you anticipate renting or buying a house for your school, first check out the following at the County Clerk's Office, or City Hall.
    a. Is the neighborhood, which you are considering, zoned for a school operation?
    b. Will the house meet the Building Code for your community?
- Usually, the cost of renovating a home to come up to code is very high. Here's what one school had to do:
    a. Rehang outside doors to open outwards: $85
    b. Construct double firewall between furnace room and adjoining classrooms: $400
    c. Install second toilet: $275
    d. Build fence to keep kids out of neighbor's yard: $325
- Check out the neighbors. Not everyone will look forward to having a school next door (see page 64). Sometimes the zoning board will require an open hearing on whether or not to let you set up business in the neighborhood. This means that all your neighbors will be invited to a hearing to voice their feelings about you. If the majority is against you, you are out. Before any such hearings, get out and ring doorbells. Rap with your neighbors, and tell them what your plans are. Remember, almost everyone is anxious about prospective change. Many people weave mysteries around unknowns, and blow them all out of proportion. Your visit can alleviate fears by providing people with concrete information.
- People get strange ideas into their heads. You may find yourself answering questions like:
    a. "Won't there be a lot of noise from the school?"
    b. "Won't children on their way to your school tramp down my flower beds?"
    c. "Isn't it true that all your students have been in trouble with the police?"
    d. "Will a school in the neighborhood depreciate our property values?"
They will probably not come out and tell exactly what's bothering them unless you probe a little. If you meet with resistance, try asking them this: "Can you tell me what it is that bothers you about having a school

in the neighborhood?" Work things out with them. Remember, it's their neighborhood, too. You're not there to overhaul their value system; you're there to run a school.

- Never lease or buy a house before fully exploring all of the above. You may otherwise end up with a house you can't use. If you're doing it through a *trustworthy* real estate agent, they will be able to help you find out about zoning. (The same will hold true of warehouses, storefronts, or any other buildings.)

SUMMARY: RENT WITH CAUTION

Watch those lease contracts. Before you sign anything check into the following:

- Is the neighborhood in which the building stands zoned for a school? (City Hall business)
- Is the building you're considering up to code for use as a school? (City Hall business)
- What will be your maintenance responsibilities? (Landlord)
- What about utilities? Will you have to pay big deposits in order to get lights, phone, gas and water hooked up? (Utility Co.)
- Are the neighbors going to hassle you? (Go door-to-door and ask if necessary.)

Understand that once you sign the lease you'll have to pay the rent for whatever period of time the lease says — even if you can't use the building. (To get legal help on drawing up a lease contract, see page 76.)

10

STEP BY STEP INSTRUCTIONS FOR INCORPORATING

LEGAL HELP

If you feel insecure about doing the corporation papers yourself, here's what I'd suggest that you do:

- Get your name cleared through the Secretary of State's Office. (see page 77)
- Type up your Articles of Incorporation and the Bylaws. (see page 126)
- Take what you've done to a lawyer you can trust; your work will save time for him, and will also tell him exactly what it is that you want. Try to get a reduced fee.

In many communities, free or low-cost legal services are available, depending on your income. Such services go by different names in different communities, so it often takes some digging to find them. They may be called by one of the following:

- Rural Legal Assistance
- Legal Aid Society
- Neighborhood Legal Services
- Judicare
- OEO Legal Services

If you can't locate someone to help you through one of these, or if you want referral to a regular lawyer, look in your yellow pages directory in the phone book under "Attorney's Reference Services." You will find several referral services listed there, any one of which will put you onto someone who can help.

GETTING THE CORPORATION TOGETHER

Incorporating and establishing your non-profit status is a long, drawn-out process. But if you take it one step at a time, using the following outline, you should have no trouble.

- *Step I: Employer Identification Number*
  Look up the telephone number, or address of your local Internal Revenue Service in your telephone directory, and ask him to send you Form SS-4. This is your application for an Employer Identification Number. You'll need it.

- *Step II: Choosing and Getting Your Name*
  Decide on some names for the school that you can live with comfortably. (see page 9) Then write to:

(If you're in California)	(For non-California)
Secretary of State	Secretary of your State
State of California	State Capitol
111 Capitol Mall	City
Sacramento, California 95814	Your State

  And say:

  > Gentlemen:
  >
  > Please advise us on the availability of the following prospective corporation names:
  >
  > a — The (name) school
  > b — The (name) school
  >
  > Thank you for your assistance.
  >
  > Yours Truly,
  > (signature)

- *Step III: Filing Form SS-4*
  Once you have received your name from the Secretary of State, fill out and send in the Employer Identification Number Application, using your new name therein.

- *Step IV: Make Your Papers*
  Turn to pages 126 and 129 in "Forms and Documents" and use the "Articles of Incorporation" and the "Bylaws" which you'll find there as models for your own papers. CAUTION: USE PICA (NOT ELITE) TYPE FACE. If possible, have these papers typed on an IBM electric typewriter, using a carbon ribbon. Then take the original typed pages to a copy service which has a Xerox 3600-III copy machine or similar machine producing *non*-shiney, clear copies, and have at least six copies made of each page. If a good quality copy machine is not available, have the typist do three originals with three *first* carbons. This will give you six fairly decent copies in all. But if you're paying for the typist, it can be expensive. These details are important: most government agencies put

everything on micro-film these days. Anything that must go in their files has to be clean, clear copy. If it's not, they'll refuse to handle it. Incidentally, California lawyers, as well as lawyers in other States, are beginning to abandon the old 8½ x 14 legal sized paper in favor of 8½ x 11. So far as I know, there aren't any government agencies refusing to handle one size or the other, but you never know. Check it out, if you can, before doing all the typing. But you'll probably be safest with the 8½ x 14. A good stationary store, preferably one frequented by lawyers, will have such information.

- *Step V: Getting the Exemption Applications*
  While you're working on the above, send to:

(In California)	(Non-California)
State of California	Your State
Franchise Tax Board	Income Tax Board
1025 P. Street	State Capitol, Your State
Sacramento, CA. 95814	

Ask them to send you Exemption Application: Form 3500 (State Tax Exemption). At the same time, have the local IRS send you an "Exemption Application, Form 1023." (Federal Tax Exemption) Getting these applications approved means your school can operate as a non-profit, tax exempt corporation.

- *Step VI: Send Your Papers Off to the Mill*
  Fill out Exemption Application, FTB-3500, using *elite* typeface. This must be done in duplicate.

  Put four copies of your Articles of Corporation, and Bylaws in a large, 8½ x 14 clasp envelope, along with the completed FTB-3500.
  Address the package to:

(For California)	(For non-California)
Secretary of State	Secretary of State
State of California	Your State Capitol
111 Capitol Mall	Your State
Sacramento, California 95814	

And include the following cover letter:

> Gentlemen:
>
> Enclosed are four copies of the creating documents for the (name) Corporation. Also enclosed are Exemption Applications to be forwarded to the Franchise Tax Board.
>
> We would like two (2) certified copies of the creating documents returned to us.

Fees are enclosed as follows:
Check to Secretary of State in the amount of $16.00.
Check to Franchise Tax Board in the amount of $10.00.

Thank you for your assistance.

Yours Truly,

(signature)

In time, you will receive some correspondence from them. If they like what you've sent, they'll give you their okay, and will forward your Exemption Application to the Franchise Tax Board. If there's something wrong, they'll tell you what it is and instruct you how to correct it.

THINGS TO REMEMBER WHEN YOU ARE INCORPORATING

The corporation's existence usually begins with the filing of the Articles of Incorporation in the office of the Secretary of the State. When the filing is acknowledged by the Secretary, a certified copy of the articles must be filed with the county clerk for the county of the principal address of the school, and in the office of the county clerk of any county in which the corporation owns real property.

In California the Secretary of State requires two copies of the articles be filed with the application and by-laws.

All states require that there be at least three directors in the corporation.

Changing the county (i.e., if you move) requires amending the articles.

Unless the articles or by-laws provide otherwise, every member of a non-profit corporation is entitled to one vote.

The specified quorum may be greater or less than a majority.

California requires that there be a president, vice president, secretary and treasurer. Most states, including California, usually allow the same person to have any two offices, but almost no state allows the president to also be the secretary.

FURTHER NOTES ON INCORPORATING

Ordinarily, the Franchise Tax Board requires a $100 deposit, refundable once you've established yourself as a non-profit organization. But this deposit is not necessary unless it's important for you to establish yourself as a corporation immediately. The only reason for speed might be if someone was waiting on you to sign a lease, or some other contractual agreement.

The two certified copies of your "creating documents" will be returned to you with the official stamp of the Secretary of State's office. Keep one set in your files, and send the other to your County Clerk's Office. Usually there's a $2.00 filing fee. You can check by phone.

- Step VII: Federal Tax Exemption

  Once you've incorporated, and have been okayed by the Secretary of State as a non-profit corporation, you can go ahead and file the Federal Exemption, Form 1023. The IRS will *not accept* this application until you're incorporated.

  More detailed information on applying for an exemption can be gotten from the IRS by asking for Form 557: How to Apply for an Exemption for Your Organization. This is the same for all states.

PUBLICATION OF NONDISCRIMINATORY POLICY

The Federal Government (IRS) is very strong on having every private school make it perfectly clear that they don't discriminate on the basis of race, creed, and so on. Unless you do it right, they won't give you a non-profit exemption status. Here's how to do it right.

- Make certain that non-discriminatory clauses are included in both the Articles of Incorporation, and the By-Laws. These clauses are included in the sample Articles and By-laws in the back of this book.
- Publish the fact of your school's non-discriminatory policy in a newspaper which is widely read by the community served by the school. (A local shopping news will not be sufficient.) It should go under "Legal Notices" in the classified section, and should read like this:

  (Name) School, (address), adopts the operational policy
  that it will not discriminate against any person on the basis of
  race, creed, color, religion, or national origin.

Get at least three copies of the newspaper in which the ad appears. Circle your ad in red pencil, and send the entire page on which it appears to the IRS, and the Franchise Tax Board, along with your exemption applications. Keep one copy for your files.

Follow these directions carefully. You won't get a non-profit status unless you do.

11

HOW TO KEEP IT ALL GOING

HASSLES AND SPLITS

Small schools of the kinds described in this book have a high mortality rate. The average life of a new school is between one and three years. In spite of this, the number of new schools in the U.S. grows each year.

I'd like to blame the high mortality rate on hassles from the authorities or the lack of funds. Small budgets and big conflicts do, of course, create frustrations and tensions. But the biggest contributions to failure come from within the schools themselves.

REALITIES VERSUS DREAMS

The idea of making your own school begins, more often than not, as a rosey notion. Then as you start filling out papers and renting space and buying insurance, and doing all the other cranky stuff you have to do to make a school go, the rosey notion begins to pale.

But somehow you push through all that, and the kids start filling the classroom. It doesn't take too long to discover that some of them don't at all coincide with your dreams of the way kids should be. Some turn out to be downright brats, others prove in the first month that they are going to need some help to learn how to cope with their new found freedoms. It's not at all like you saw in your mind-movies. After the first month of school, three parents have complained that the school allows too much freedom, and three others have complained that your school is too rigid. Still others are demanding that you teach more academics, while more are arguing that subject matter should be dropped altogether. It's impossible to satisfy everyone, so you try to just ride out the storm. Tensions grow, and by the end of the first year the school is split between two groups: those who want more "structure" and those who want less.

UTOPIAN PITFALLS

The sources of our failures may very well be the same ones that give impetus to the movement, that being that we are all, to some degree, utopian in our thinking. This means that:

- At the point when our dreams go sour, or appear to go sour, our reflex is to flee the site of our disillusionment.
- Instead of sticking around and learning how to solve problems, we strike out for new territories in search of a new dream.

We need tools to help us keep going.

PROBLEM SOLVING

Problem solving is a skill which is learned. It is also an attitude. People who embody this attitude will:

- recognize when something isn't working right, even when it's his own fault
- try to figure out what's wrong
- seek better ways of doing something that isn't working

Don't confuse "problem solvers" with "reformers." Reformers seek out problems in order to demonstrate *that they know better.* Reformers seldom stick around to enjoy the fruits of their labors, because their motives are not pleasure but proving that they know better than anyone else.

A person develops a problem-solving attitude by:

- acknowledging that he is not helpless to affect change by creating something new
- taking the responsibility for finding workable solutions
- asking for advice and assistance from others when he can't solve the problem all by himself
- discovering that it is better to make things more comfortable than to complain that they're not.

HIERARCHIES AND OTHER DIRTY WORDS

As soon as you move beyond the simplicity of the Minimal School, you face the problems of developing workable systems for the necessary division of labor and responsibility. Along with the division of labor will come the creation of a hierarchy. Unless all this is approached in a direct manner, a "pecking order" takes over, with power struggles and injured egos building to create a major crisis.

So approach this problem openly. Schedule regular school meetings which include everyone that has anything to do with the day to day operation of the school.

Use the meetings to discuss the problem of divvying up the various tasks which need be done to keep the school going (see page 65). Soon you'll begin to see that someone has to oversee the whole operation, that this job needs doing as much as sweeping the floors needs doing. It's not just an honor; it's a skill requiring a tremendous outlay of energy.

WHAT DOES A LEADER LOOK LIKE?

Here's what I think a good leader should be able to do:
- Solve problems
- Oversee the entire operation
  - a. How the kids are doing
  - b. How the teachers are doing
  - c. How the parents are doing
  - d. How the janitor is doing
  - e. How the neighbors are doing
  - f. How the landlord is doing
  - g. How the authorities are doing
- Be able to:
  - a. make decisions
  - b. give orders
  - c. take orders
  - d. fill in for anyone who doesn't show up for work
  - e. help his people when they're in trouble
  - f. listen to everybody and try out their ideas
- Understand the difference between democratic processes and
  - a. subtle power struggles
  - b. grandstanding
  - c. talking because you don't want to act
  - (These three points are all too often defended as "democratic processes.")
- Be able to get things done where others fail.
- Respect the rights of other people.
- Recognize his own limits as well as those of others around him, and not

put down or feel put down because of them. (Remember, it's not doing everything well that makes a person effective; it's being able to get help when you can't that does the trick.)

If you're hiring a leader, you'll have to make up a list of questions which cover the above points and then get those questions answered when you're interviewing. If you're choosing a leader from an existing group, spend some time discussing the above points — plus lots more that you'll come up with — and only then go on to electing a leader.

LEADER-NON-LEADER DYNAMICS

The leader-non-leader dynamic depends on a delicate balance based on mutual respect and trust. Without a full understanding of this dynamic, you can have tyranny, which means chaos which means discomfort and lots of negative energy.

How to establish that balance is a subject which can take up at least the space of four books the size of this one. So I will do little more here than to suggest a path to follow, and point out that the leader-non-leader dynamic must become part of the curriculum of every small school.

THE LEADER'S FUNCTION

The leader's function is to get things done. If he doesn't do that he's no leader at all.

The leader gets things done by:
- Doing it himself.
- Assigning the responsibility of completing a task to someone else.
- Following the progress of job assignments to see that they get done, and to give or get further assistance if the person to whom he's given an assignment needs help completing the job.

THE NON-LEADER'S FUNCTION

Non-leaders have more power than leaders. Although leaders can give orders, they cannot make the work get done right. Furthermore, if non-leaders fear their leaders, and are afraid to leave their jobs, they can simply do their jobs badly, and thus screw up the whole operation. Any such actions can make the leader look bad. Organized labor proved all this to be true.

More often than not, the leader's powers are limited to how much the non-leaders are willing to allow him. When things are bad, and no one wants to take responsibility for what's going on, leaders *assert* power but are unable to get things done. Frustration goes on the rise, and things get worse until there's either a purge or a new leader comes forward who has the support of the non-leaders.

Since the non-leader does hold so much power, it is important to recognize his functions. Here's a rudimentary list:

- He recognizes the acknowledged leader.
- He gets deep personal satisfaction from doing his own job rather than coveting the leader's position.
- He does not spend his time claiming that he could be a better leader than the present one, but offers his ideas for improvement to the leader.
- He has the courage to demand a new leader when the old one has ceased to do his job well.

But remember, our ideal non-leader only exists when the leader is doing his job well.

MODEL CONFLICTS

Here are some model conflicts which involve leader-non-leader struggles and which nearly all organizations seem to face at one time or another. They are:

- Some members push for one man, one vote absolute democracy — how can the group function in democratic chaos?
- Direct disagreement among members over policy, curriculum, or hiring teachers builds tension.
- Individuals who disagree with the recognized leader slowly coalesce around a new and outspoken member, eventually polarizing the organization into two or more groups.

MONTHLY RAP SESSIONS

Regularly scheduled rap sessions, designated as the time to air complaints and discuss individual problems and conflicts, will greatly expand the possibility for continuing the school. During these meetings, be open, direct, and honest. Here are five model questions to ask:

- Does anyone have any complaints?
- Does anyone have a major beef with anyone else? If so, let's have the courage to open it up to the group.
- Does anyone have any ideas for solving the problem of_____?
- How can we maintain a democratic atmosphere and still get the work done that needs being done?
- Does anyone have any complaints about our leader?

EDUCATIONAL PHILOSOPHY

Developing an educational philosophy should be a group process, and an ongoing and ever-changing thing. Exploring your own philosophy of education so that your fellow teachers, parents, and students can agree with or refute you, will bring the school together.

In order to develop an educational philosophy on the basis of group processes, you'll want to start with specifics. Deal with real issues in real classrooms, not fuzzy dreams of the way things *ought* to be. Here are five sample questions to deal with:

- How do you distinguish between high spirits and hysteria in children?
- How do children learn how to read?
- Should you "set limits" for people?
- What stress should we place on subject matter?
- How do children know when they're learning?

I deal with many of these questions in the section called, WHAT I THINK AND FEEL ABOUT TEACHING (see page 92). When you're reading through that section, don't read it as gospel. Take my comments as though they are my contribution to your next group meeting. What I say there is simply part of an ongoing dialogue; it is process, not a static object.

SPECIAL PROBLEMS NO-ONE LIKES TO FACE

All schools have to face unpleasant tasks such as the following:

- Reprimanding parents for non-payment of fees, and making collections
- dropping children of parents who refuse to pay
- deciding what to do with an overly agressive child
- deciding what to do with children who remain unhappy and withdrawn, and who don't like the school
- deciding what to do for children with emotional problems which the school can't handle
- deciding what to do for children with health problems which the parents refuse to acknowledge
- deciding what to do for children who are constantly hurting other children

These problems, and others like them, should be dealt with in meetings called especially to make decisions on such issues. What course of action to take will, in most cases, be the work of several, rather than one person. However you deal with them, whatever your decisions, you will definitely need to make it clear to every staff member that you do have a way of sharing the burden. Doing nothing, then allowing problems to pile up, often leads to crises which divide the school.

INTERVIEWING ADULTS

Try to start out with new people on a ground of understanding one another. It'll save enormous hassles later on. Initial interviewing, though not infallable, provides a tool for doing this. There are two kinds of interviews:

- parents
- employees

Begin an interview by telling about yourself:

- Describe your own position in relationship to the school
  a. are you a parent with responsibility for interviewing?
  b. are you the principal of the school?
  c. other?
- Describe the school
  a. how many students
  b. the age range of the students
  c. a brief rundown of the school philosophy
- Money matters
  a. how the school is supported (tuitions, donations, etc.)
  b. cost of tuition (for parents)
  c. how much you can pay (for prospective employees)

Get all this down to a five minute statement. It can be done by narrowing yourself down to essentials. If necessary, do it on paper first, then discard the paper before the interview. Don't attempt to cover everything. People being interviewed are usually nervous, and they won't remember much more than five minutes worth of information anyway.

After your introductory statement, ask the person being interviewed "Does this sound interesting to you?" If they answer no, do not try to sell them on any of your ideas. You might be able to talk them into agreeing with you, but the agreement will be only temporary and will result in hassles later on, maybe after you've hired them or accepted their kids into your school. So don't get into all that, just see them politely to the door, and thank them for coming in. If their answer is more positive, continue the interview. You'll need to find out:

- Their past experience
  a. experience with other schools
  b. employment experience if you're interviewing for that
- Their philosophy of education
- When they can start, and whether or not their starting date will work out with your own needs/plans.

If you get through these first parts okay, loosen up. Take them into the classroom to talk, with the kids milling around them. Here's what you'll find out there:

- Do they appear nervous or relaxed with the kids?

• Do the kids relate to them openly or with mistrust?

Spend at least fifteen minutes in the classroom. Then retreat to a quiet corner with them, and ask this very important question:

"How does our classroom make you feel?"

This question will probably make them uneasy. But insist on an answer since the answer will tell more about the person you're interviewing than anything you've asked them thus far. From that point on, it's up to you to make a choice. For the most part, you'll be relying on your own impressions of the person. You'll want to trust those impressions because in the intimacy of a small school your feelings about the people you work with will often prove more important than how many years of experience the people show on their application forms. Trust your gut feelings.

INTERVIEWING KIDS

It's important to meet prospective students before accepting them into your school. The best way to do this is to invite them into the classroom. Go around with them and show them what kind of stuff you have, and how things work. Here are some rules to follow:

• DON'T introduce the new kid to anyone. Introductions make kids feel obligated to make friends immediately. Kids don't do it that way. They'll play with another kid for hours, and sometimes days before they learn each other's names.

• DON'T ask them questions, especially not ones like:
   a. Do you like school?
   b. What's your favorite subject?

• Most of what you say should be in the form of simple, declarative sentences like:
   a. Here's our book corner.
   b. Let me show you our playground.
   c. Look at this microscope slide.

When it's done this way, most kids will get involved in the activities. My experience has been that they get so much into it that they don't want to leave when it's time to go. At any rate, you'll be able to see how the kid functions in your environment, and this experience will provide you with impressions on which to base your decision of whether or not to take him into the school.

Focus on your feelings about the prospective student; i.e., if he was withdrawn, did you feel that the school would eventually be able to draw him out? If he was overly agressive and "grabby" did you feel the other kids would be able to handle this okay? Remember, children are often quite tense coming into a new situation, especially a new school, and can act pretty screwy even though they may prove to be quite happy and relaxed with the new situation after a few days of living with it. So take this into account.

LEAVING YOURSELF AN OUT

When you accept a new child into the school, do it this way:
1. Get the parent and child in the same room and paying attention to you.
2. Turn to the child and say, "I'd like to have you come to our school. We'll see how it goes for two weeks. Then you can tell me how you like it."

The words in number 2 are important. Notice they don't imply "We're putting you on trial." If anything, they're weighted to the other side, like: "you try *us* for two weeks." The words are designed to make an agreement on positive grounds, with the child's judgement being respected.

After this, turn to the parent and say:

"Let's set up a meeting with the three of us two weeks after Johnny starts to school here. What time would work out for you?"

This arrangement will allow you to give each other a real tryout, and will also leave everyone a clear path for avoiding unworkable relationships should it prove that the school and Johnny just aren't compatible.

A SURVIVAL KIT FOR INTERVIEWING AUTHORITIES

Some local school districts pay attention to private school operations, some don't. Should you get a visit from yours, you will want to know what they'll be looking for. Here are some of the main questions and answers:

Q:Who are the people in charge of your school?

A:(Show them your affidavit [page 114], or give them the information that it contains.)

Q:Who are your teachers?

A:We have (number) teachers, who are supervised by (name), who is a credentialed (or experienced) teacher.

Q:How do you keep your attendance records?

A:Daily attendance is recorded by the individual teachers, and is recorded in our office attendance files once per month. Here are our office attendance files. (Get out your monthly attendance records and hand them to the school authority.)

Q:What is your curriculum?

A:We parallel public school curriculum, so that children transferred back to public school will be at a place similar to their public school peers. (Remember, you will be required to teach the subjects outlined in the "Summary," page 123. Make a list of these courses, and keep them on hand to recite back to the authorities should you forget what they are!) In addition, we like to follow "Basic Course of Study." (Keep a copy of this in reach. See page 16.)

Q:Do you have any children enrolled who are under four years and nine months of age?

A:No, we do not enroll preschool-aged children in our school.

Q:What provisions do you have for fire drills?

A:We follow this plan. (Show them a typewritten sheet of instructions for getting the kids out of the building in the event of fire. It should be orderly, and realistic. This plan should be fastened to a wall for everyone to see. Local fire departments often have "Emergency Procedures" cards, which give details for what to do in case of natural disasters: hurricanes, tornadoes, etc. You can get copies of these for the asking, from your local Fire Chief. Having one or more up on strategic walls in your school will impress the authorities, and may very well come in handy some day.)

Q:How do you handle emergencies?

A:We keep an Emergency Information file (See page 67) with a card for each child. In this way, we can contact the parent immediately in the event of serious injury or illness. If the parent cannot be contacted in time, we take the child to (name) Emergency Hospital. We of course have a first aid kit (show them) which is properly supplied as recommended in the Education Code. (See page 121)

In the course of such a visit, put the authority in the position of helping you. If they feel that you consider them a friend they are more likely to make "recommendations" – rather than flat out hassle you. Here's how to do this:

Tell them that you are in the process of creating an "open classroom" situation, but that your desire is to parallel public school curriculum plans wherever possible. Ask them if it's possible for them to tell you what "achievement" tests are used by the public schools themselves. You may even be able to get copies of these tests (See page 99) to look over, giving you a further indicator of the authorities' expectations.

If you're still in the first stages of forming a school, and have no more than one or two students, though you've filed the affidavit properly, here's what to say:

We're just beginning to get our school together. At present we don't really have that much to show since we are holding classes in public places such as parks, museums, libraries, and in student's homes. We are, however, keeping attendance records and are basing our curriculum on "Basic Course of Study."

Whenever interviewing authorities, don't put them in the position of being your enemy. Rather, put them in the position of "advising" you. Understand that you don't have to do what they tell you: at least not in most cases. But they do have a much bigger machine behind them than you do. So keep in mind that if you put them in the position of being the enemy, that automatically puts you in the position of being the "victim" – and that's a clearcut energy ripoff. You'll discover that you do have control over this situation if you can learn to greet authorities cheerfully and openly, and to ask them questions which they'll enjoy answering.

Keep cool. Remember, the authorities are human too. It's your job to reach that humaness.

FUND RAISING

Here's a list of tried and true fund raising schemes which many schools report to be worth the effort:

- Flea markets
- Rock Concerts
- Bake Sales
- Booths in Local Fairs
- Annual School Festival
- Adult Education Classes using school facilities in the evening

Some schools get into government grants, but as soon as you do that you're right back into the system again, with inspectors coming around to find out how their money is being spent. But if that's your bag, you can find out all you need to know about current government grants, and how to get them from the following people:

Grant Data Quarterly
10835 Santa Monica Blvd.
Los Angeles, California 90025

The cost of a subscription is between thirty and fifty dollars per year, and that includes some extras besides the quarterlies themselves. True, there's a lot of money out there begging for a home.

12

WHAT I THINK AND FEEL ABOUT TEACHING

THE LEARNING PROCESSES ARE CONTAINED IN THE SELF

As the child learns, he may be quite unaware of learning. Seemingly the skills he has at any moment he has always had, and for this reason he may take for granted his power to learn. And so a skillful teacher might point this out to him, remarking as the child learns that there was once a time when he had not known what he now knows: proof of his power to learn and evidence that the learning processes are contained in the self. To point out to him, for example, that he once did not know how to speak but that now he does, and that he has "taught himself" a great many things besides, will help to make him aware of his great strength as a learner.

WHAT LEARNING IS AND ISN'T

The teacher doesn't instill knowledge in the student. The teacher can only make certain knowledge AVAILABLE, but it is up to the child to familiarize himself with it, and (perhaps) incorporate it into his being.

When the child's memory becomes the teacher's chief target, then whatever faith the child may have in his own capacity to learn is undermined.

LEARNING TO LEARN IS THE KEY

Most of us, I would guess, have been pretty solidly conditioned to associate education with the 3 R's and flag saluting, and if we know better intellectually, old reflexes persist and tend to shake our confidence where building something better is concerned. So every morning, do as I do, and repeat to yourself fifty times: EDUCATION AIN'T THE THREE R's. Maybe it'll help.

Learning to learn is the key. And if your kids don't know how now it's only because their knowledge of these primal processes have been chased into hiding either by you or by too much public schooling. If you're to blame don't withdraw in despair, because after a few months, or weeks, or days of working closely with your kid you might just figure out where you went wrong, and you'll probably start remembering what happened to you back there in your own blackboard days, and soon you'll be hearing the primal message loud and clear and bouncing back and forth between you and the kid. Learning to learn is the key.

GIVE WHAT YOU LOVE THE MOST

Attitude tells all. It's the master teacher. If, for example, a child is confronted by an uptight teacher whose motors burned up or blew out thirty years before, teaching, let's say reading, the kid isn't going to learn reading half so well as he'll learn uptightness. In other words, if the mill is rusty and the engines dead, you're not going to take your business there even when the sign on the door says COME ON IN. And that is why kids don't learn at old P.S. 169.

One of the better teachers I know used to knit in class, partly because it kept her cool in the midst of children's chaos, partly because she liked the feel and color of the linked cords of wool, but mostly because she knew that her enjoyment and involvement was transmitted to the children as they went about their business of learning whatever they needed to learn. Lax? Very! Under her tutorage an eight year old girl got into reading for the first time in her life. What happened was that the teacher created the attitude of involvement and pleasure in the process of doing something, and the child, who had been struggling unsuccessfully with reading for several years picked up a germ of confidence or fun or whatever, and got with it. The teacher, of course, did answer questions when asked, but that wasn't her strongest point, obviously, since other teachers had been answering questions for the little girl for quite a few years with no results. Not that reading is all that important: but apparently it was what this particular little girl at that particular time did want to learn.

RHYTHMS IN LEARNING

Wait for times when your student becomes deeply engrossed in his learning, and then guardedly watch his face, his hands, his body. Concentrate on seeing him as his own person, a person very separate from you, with a huge gambit of capacities for seeing, feeling, tasting, hearing, intuiting, figuring things out, running, walking, loving, hating, showing compassion, indifference, eventually procreating.

As you watch him notice how his eyes move, his mouth, his hands, his arms and legs. You will see that learning involves his entire being. Often a child's body will express a rhythm, either in small muscle movements or large, rhythms which go along with learning and which will begin to express a consistency from one learning period to the next. Learn to recognize these rhythms, but don't force them, since part of learning to learn is finding one's own pace.

FORCE FEEDINGS

... usually cause vomiting in the infant, and are one of the best methods available for teaching defensiveness, distrust, and resentment to the child.

Before attempting to teach anything, meditate on what your kid has already learned, both the good and the bad, and do this consciously, deliberately, say twenty minutes every evening before you go to bed, and when the house is quiet, and when no other demands are being made on you. Sit down with a cup of tea, in an undisturbed corner, and allow that knowledge to come through. What your child has already accomplished should inspire you to believe in him. (Remember, even the "bad" things that he's learned are evidence of his huge capacity for learning!) If this doesn't immediately inspire you, keep on until it does. But come to think of it, some people are never inspired by such things, and if you're one of these you should definitely find another activity for yourself, one in which you can find gratification. Find your child another teacher. You'll both be happier with each other.

CONSEQUENCES OF TAKING YOUR CHILD
OUT OF PUBLIC SCHOOL

Consequences?! If you're still thinking in those terms, you'd better put this book down. Of course there are consequences! Leaving Maggie's farm ain't easy!

WHAT TO TEACH

Glibly, the answer is: "Whatever the kid wants to learn." But if your child has already learned the responses necessary for survival in the traditional classroom, he will need a bridge to that place where he will want to learn. So I'd suggest beginning with an hour's formal learning period each day, an hour which should be measured by the clock, preferably a clock which the child can watch. If an hour is really too long, try thirty minutes, but still use the clock. If nothing else, he will learn a little something about measuring time.

During the measured hour, tell your student that he may do any kind of schoolwork that he wishes to do. A younger child will often like to write "dirty" words, words which he has probably been prevented from using, although he has no doubt learned their great power as a tool for shocking adults at the Super Market. At any rate, practice at writing such words may become one of his first big acts of rebellion, directed toward experiencing his separateness from others, and it will help him to build confidence in his capacity for independent learning. When we started my seven year old son on such a plan, he filled an entire notebook with a thousand "FUCK's," nearly two weeks, or fourteen hours of work, before he asked how to write his own last name. He not only got very caught up in the learning process, he broke the mystery of the word's shock value, and has since used the word only quite legitimately — as an exclamation of anger or awe, and to discuss sex.

During the child's schoolwork hour the teacher should not enforce any particular labors, but should leave all that to the kid. If he sits and moans for an hour that's okay, because once he learns that it's going to happen whether he fusses or not, he'll begin to search for ways to amuse himself, to "pass the time," and this search for amusement is the teacher's sign that the kid's ready to learn how to learn.

The first signs of interest in learning may come in negative forms: "Aw, all I ever get to do is sit here!" To which the teacher might respond: "Well, what would you like to do while you're sitting there?" If the answer is TV, forget it, and don't even turn on good educational programs during this hour. (While we're on the subject, I have an idea that "Popeye" is more relevant for a child exploring behavior with his peers than is "Sesame Street," though I can't find much to recommend either of them.) Even at its best TV teaches a passive attitude, and what you're after in the formalized learning hour is the child's aggressive engagement of his capacities and energies with the world around him. Be persistent, calm, and above all have faith in him.

If the child asks you to read to him, do it, but tell him that you will read only for fifteen minutes, and tell him that he must pick the book. This accomplishes two things: it puts the stress on his making his own choices, and it signals him that you will participate within certain limits. The same goes for games — checkers, chess, that sort of thing.

As the child learns that the burden of what to do with his hour rests on his shoulders, he will begin to find things to do, if only out of a simple sense of survival. He may draw, if he wishes, or take apart an old clock, do jigsaw puzzles — which incidentally are great for teaching spatial relationships and shape recognition, the rudiments of reading and writing — or any number of things which require the engagement of his aggressive human capacities.

By now the teacher will have gotten in touch with the sense of wonder at the child's past accomplishments, and will remember also the power of sincere exclamations of encouragement. College Ed courses tell you to use something called "positive reinforcement" which is mostly bullshit, because it quickly becomes used as a form of bribery, the old carrot at the donkey's nose routine. The point is that if you're in touch with your student you know that he will do things which will inspire your spontaneous expressions of approval and even delight in his accomplishments; you don't have to invent them. You need only free yourself to express the spirit of such moments.

At four years of age, my son used to put on his nursery school teacher by handing her mindless scribbles — at a time in his life when he was drawing motorcycles and people — in order to get her to go into her "Oh, that's very nice!" routine. I put an end to it when he took me into his class for the sole purpose of demonstrating the entire phenomenon for me. I congratulated him for figuring it out, and on the way home we discussed how teachers were taught such things in college but that it probably meant she didn't know her students very well. My son ended the discussion by saying, "I'll draw real pictures tomorrow." And he did.

LEARNING TO READ

Reading is not so hard to teach or learn if you simply remember that your student already knows how to make the sounds and that in order to read he must convert the "heard" signals to "seen" signals. This involves discovering a decoding system based on the principal that lines arranged in certain ways stand for sounds that he already hears and makes.

Teach him how to write his name, and always have a bunch of big letters knocking around for him to feel, trace, make words with. Most good toy stores can sell you a set of 2 inch plastic letters for about three dollars or less. Wooden ones are nicer but usually are more expensive and harder to find.

Have a lot of good books around, with exciting stories the kids like.

Don't come on too strong about this reading thing. Living in a verbal culture, we tend to get panicked about our kids not learning to read at an early age. But there really does seem to be a time when a child is ready to learn to read, and that age varies greatly, causing teachers and parents untold anxiety.

When a child does begin to read, help him out when he can't decode a word. Don't make him sweat over sounding it out. If he could, he wouldn't ask you for help. Relax! It's a long, slow, building process, so pace it out, respecting where the student is at every moment.

After intensive learning periods, pause, let it rest for a day, two days, a week. The various elements of complex ideas need to shake around in the brain before they incorporate to make a whole. When you get back to it, the progress made is often astounding. Practice goes on silently in the brain. Drills and tests only prohibit this process from taking place.

WORKBOOKS

They're okay, especially the cheap ones that you can buy at dime stores. But if you're going to use them, pick some that are fun for kids to do, with places for drawing and writing. There are some pretty fair workbooks on the New Math, published by Dell, which I bought for myself when I wanted to learn it.

BOUNDARIES OF ACTION

Perhaps the most difficult thing that teachers and parents face is the business of discovering, defining, and teaching the boundaries of action: i.e., how far a child can go before he endangers himself or distresses the adult. Mostly, kids don't recognize their own limits, and shouldn't be expected to know yours without your telling them. It confuses them when you express discomfort about their actions without telling them why their actions are upsetting you. Let them know simply but clearly where you're at.

After you practice discovering and defining the boundaries of action with a child, he will respect the process, and will even be grateful to you for making things clear to him. Through this interaction, he learns how his actions affect other people, and that the world is not indifferent to him at all. His life has significance in relation to other humans, and he begins to know how to recognize the myriad of ways in which he can move the world.

BOOKLIST

1. *Play Therapy,* Virginia Axline, Ballantine $1.25
2. *Teaching Montessori in the Home,* Elizabeth Hainstock, Random $6.95
3. *Human Teaching for Human Learning,* George Isaac Brown, Viking $8.50
4. *Schools Without Failure,* William Glasser, Harper $4.95
5. *Put your Mother On The Ceiling,* Richard de Mille, Walker $3.95
6. *In The Early World,* Elwyn S. Richardson, Pantheon $7.95
7. *Towards A Visual Culture,* Caleb Cattegno, Avon $1.65
8. *How To Parent,* Dr. Fitzhugh Dodson, N.A.L. $1.25
9. *How To Live With Your Special Child,* George von Hilsheimer, Acropolis $7.50

13

WHAT TO DO IF YOUR SCHOOL FOLDS

ANTICIPATE THE FUTURE

It can, and does happen that the small school folds after the first year of operation — and for any of a number of reasons, some of which this book discusses. Although I try to provide information which will assist you in minimizing the chances of this happening, you may still want to consider the alternatives beyond the alternatives.

If the school itself doesn't fail, but you find yourself the "odd man out"as the result of disagreements on policy or educational philosophy, you will probably feel frustrated, angry and disillusioned. You may also feel anxious for your child, like, "What's to become of him now?" These feelings, though normal enough, and certainly to be expected under the circumstances, can still hang you up and cause you to make decisions which you may later have second thoughts about.

There are a number of alternatives to consider. You can:
- Put your child back in public school.
- Put your child in a different alternative school.
- Start another school of your own.
- Educate your child at home.

Since these concerns do affect most people in the alternative school scene, you will be able to find support in doing the following:

1. Make "What to do if the school folds" the subject of school meetings.
2. Establish people to people contacts with other schools which might be able

to take your child, or children, into their school should yours fold.

3. Have meetings, parties, informal get-togethers, flea markets and other fund-raising projects, with other schools in order to establish comaradery: that's called, "Getting a little help from your friends."

4. Work for, or help start an "Education Switchboard." All you need is a telephone in someone's home or school, to provide a central number for people to call in order to get information about alternative schools, and to co-ordinate the efforts of all new schools in the community. The "Switchboard" is also excellent for putting together a "Substitute Teachers" list to serve all alternative schools in the community.

The farther you get into it, the more important an Education Switchboard will become. More and more people are finding it an excellent means of getting together for rap sessions — the key to finding effective solutions to problems faced by small schools. You'll be able to use this structure for everything from resolving personal conflicts in regard to school matters to forming joint fund raising campaigns. Remember, sharing resources is what community is all about.

With these tools at your disposal, you'll still have to make a decision about what to do next (if your school folds), but at least you'll have a great amount of information at your fingertips to assist you in making that decision. Let's hope you'll never have to use it.

HOW TO GET YOUR KID BACK IN PUBLIC SCHOOL

You may want to have a school of your own only until your child reaches the junior high or high school age, after which you'll want to transfer him back to public school. This can be done.

Most school districts require that a child take tests to evaluate his general abilities as they relate to others in his own peer group. This is done regularly, for both their continuing students, and for students transferring in. It is not a pass or fail situation they're after so much as a matter of assessing how the kid fits into their program. Often these tests are administered by an independent testing company; the school does not do their own evaluations. Tests are given for all grade levels, from first grade on.

If you have done everything necessary to become an approved school, there's no reason in the world that you can't contract with the same testing company as the public school. The tests will show you exactly what your kids have to learn in order to fit into the public school program.

The following is a dependable testing company. They do a large percentage of the public school evaluations in the U.S., and they advertise that they will design an evaluation program to meet your particular needs:

Science Research Associates, Inc.
259 East Erie Street
Chicago, Illinois 60611

Tell them that you are interested in having an "SRA Testing Program" for your school. Once you discover what the public schools require, you can either "coach" your kids to pass the tests, or establish a curriculum to teach the same subject matter as the public schools. This can be accomplished the year prior to transferring, or can be continuous through all the grades taught at your school. Here again, "Basic Course of Study" (see page 16) will help you.

These evaluation procedures are as common in other states as they are in California. SRA does their thing anywhere.

TRANSFER TO COLLEGE FROM PRIVATE HIGH SCHOOLS

It is common practice, especially with expensive, system-wise private schools, to coach their students in taking and passing college entrance exams. In "high society" schools, it's done so that they can advertise how many of their students get into college every year. These exams are, of course, arbitrary to begin with, and this practice only points out that the exams are not only arbitrary, they're downright absurd. There's nothing to prevent any school from coaching for exams, using copies of the tests which have been begged, borrowed, or pirated from some college or university. Of course, the better schools don't do it that way; they buy their tests from a reputable testing company. (See page 99.) It's the system-wise thing to do!

OR, you can simply use the coaching materials of either of the following:

* American College Testing Program Exam—$4.00
  ARCO
  219 Park Avenue South
  New York, N.Y. 10003

* How To Prepare For College Entrance Exams—$4.00
  Barons Educational Series, Inc.
  113 Crossways Park Drive
  Woodbury, New York 11797

These books lay out a whole study plan for you.

14

LOOSE ENDS

BASIC ANXIETY QUESTIONS

- Q: Will my child feel separated and alienated from his peer group if I take him out of public schools?
  A: Maybe, But if you include him in the preliminary planning of your school he will develop his own understanding of what's going on, and will be *a part of something new* instead of being simply *separated from something familiar.* Then, as your school takes shape and other children come into it, your child will establish friendships within a new peer group.
- Q: Should I try to explain to my children why the public schools are bad?
  A: No, not if they are younger than ten or twelve. Younger children should be allowed the luxury of believing that adults can be trusted. When you're in the position a younger child is in, not knowing too much about the world yet, and being dependent on grown-ups to help you figure it out, you need the security of this phantasy. Don't undermine it any more than is necessary. Rather teach him that you are creating something better than the public schools have to offer. Don't dwell on the fact of its "badness." One of the lessons we've learned from the "alternative" dialogue is that energy in whatever form is always energy; using energy to express anger and discontent is a diversion from the business of building something that will satisfy.

- Q: Will my child learn how to read if he is not in the public schools?

  A; Yes. In the Infant Schools in England they've had a great deal of success with their students learning how to read pretty much on their own. They do not *teach* reading. They make reading *available* to the children in the form of story books. A reading corner and many, many books are always within reach. There are no textbooks, no primers, no formalized lesson periods. Walking into an Infant School is reported to be a very unsettling experience for American educators; they see what appears to be chaos and teachers who aren't particularly attentive to the group action (or don't appear to be). Yet, children are learning more in the Infant Schools than in any other educational plan going in the English-speaking countries. These Infant Schools, by the way, are operated by what in England is equivalent to our Public School System. They appear to be at least twenty years ahead of us in public education. What they know is that learning to read is a very personalized process for each child. Some children learn to read at the age of three and four, while others don't learn till they're nine or ten. There's a time when each child is *ready* to read, and that time should be respected. Making books available, accessible, is the best way I know to "teach" reading. Children don't need *to be taught* so much as they need *to be allowed to learn.* (See page 92 for further discussion.)

- Q: My child is "undisciplined" in everything he does, just doesn't seem to want to apply himself to anything. Won't a "free school" atmosphere only aggravate this?

  A: It will probably aggravate it less than the traditional public school classroom does. Apropos of this, I'd say that *discipline* is not willfully imposed, but is something that develops out of a deep interest in doing something. That's as true for children as it is of adults. I remember a field trip to a newspaper plant when I was ten or eleven years old. I had a paper route at the time, and the trip was sponsored by the newspaper people to "motivate" newsboys, I suppose. Well, the trip turned me onto writing and reading, for some mysterious reason, and very much turned me off to delivering newspapers. I became the "most disciplined" eleven year old reader and writer in the neighborhood — and, ironically, began to flunk my English classes at school. And the more "disciplined" I became in reading and writing, the less "disciplined" I became as a newsboy, until I at last lost the route. The "free school" approach to education encourages children to explore, since exploration often leads a child to discover something that truly interests him and to which he will "apply" himself ardently. Discipline, like love, develops from within, and cannot be successfully imposed from the outside.

- Q: What is "an approved curriculum"?

  A: The term "approved curriculum" has been used a lot in the years since the rising popularity of small private schools as alternatives to public education. The term has been used mostly by school administrators as a means of harrassing parents turning to private education, the intent being to imply that they're doing something illegal or bad for their children if the school doesn't have this so-called "approved curriculum." If your school is meeting the requirements of the education code (see pages 7, 114, and 117), your school is legally "approved." However, most school districts do have a curriculum plan which may or may not coincide with yours; this plan is the "approved curriculum." But the fact that they are doing it does not make it right. If you're interested in finding out what an "approved curriculum" looks like, get a copy of "Basic Course of Study" (see page 16.)

- Q: What about High School Graduation?
  A: If your high school meets the standards for a high school curriculum (see page 124), that school can issue a diploma. If not, there's a provision in the education laws of all states for getting a high school diploma through taking an "equivalency examination." Get a book called, "G.E.D. High School Equivalency Diploma Tests," published by: ARCO, 219 Park Avenue South, New York, New York 10003. This book tells everything that you need to know on the subject, and is a "complete study guide for scoring high." This company also publishes books on career guidance, and on passing tests for everything from Able Seaman to Science Scholarship Exams, and Teacher License exams. They list about 350 books like this. Send for their catalog.

- Q: What about college?
  A: A friend of mine who runs a little junior high school in Marin County answers this question with a counter-question; "What about *now?*" His response does, of course, imply an important truth: that the future is nothing if the present is empty. But perhaps the question deserves a more direct response. *The kind of education which this book deals with does not have, as one of its goals, preparation for college.* However, with less than a year of coaching, any kid with an average intelligence can pass a college entrance exam. Copies of college entrance exams are available for study (see page 99.) And then there's what's known as the GED materials which are designed for coaching for high school graduation equivalency.

- Q: What about Academics?
  A: There's only one way I can answer this, that being that I can see no correlation between academic achievement and "success in life." I do, however, believe it's important to expose a child to a great variety of interests: literature, science, arts, music, etc. From these, he can make his own choices. If your kid becomes interested in chemistry, for example,

by all means put him in a position to explore that interest. The child who can identify with and imitate someone practicing in the child's field of interest is most likely to deepen his exploration of himself and his desire for academic pursuit.

- Q: But what about employment in later years? Don't most jobs require advanced degrees?

A: Civil Rights reforms in the past decade have managed to prove, in many cases, that the diploma requirements for college and employment are discriminatory, excluding people who are otherwise qualified. Many jobs, including most Civil Service positions, now carry with them an equivalency clause, meaning that if you can prove yourself capable of performing the job, you must be considered for it.

The Federal Government publishes a bulletin called: "Jobs for which a high school education is preferred but not essential." You get it from:

U.S. Department of Labor
Bureau of Labor Statistics
Washington, D.C. 20212

or your local Dept. of Labor branch, a visit to which, by the way, would make a fine field trip.

SOFT REVOLUTION TECHNIQUES

- If you believe your kids are important, but can't see your way clear to taking them out of public school, you can do your part in dismantling the public school system in order to clear the way for something better, by *voting against all bond issues.* This is a silent protest, expressed in the voting booth, but if you want to make more noise about what you're doing and why, write a letter to your Superintendent of Schools and tell him that you have and will continue to vote against new bond issues until significant changes are made in the schools.
- If you want to go further, keep your child out of school on an *unexcused absence basis* for at least two days per week. Local school districts get funds from the state based on hours of student attendance. A low attendance report means that less money will be coming into the local school district from the state.
- Go even further; organize parent groups to do these things as a group. Imagine the power of 1,000 signatures from parents stating that they would no longer vote for any school bond issues!

A WORD ABOUT FOOD

Having once set up and supervised a hot lunch program for 100 preschool children, my advice to small schools is to stay out of complex food operations altogether. Health Department regulations are really tough, and meeting those regulations can be expensive. Co-ordinating food buying and nutrition planning, plus worries about major and minor food poisoning, add up to a scene requiring as much energy as setting up the school itself.

What do you do instead? Have the kids bring lunches from home. You can expand on this by getting a refrigerator and having fresh milk in those half-pint containers for the kids. And in the cold season, you can put on a pot of good soup or hot chocolate.

Learning about food is important and it's something that most kids will enjoy getting into. So don't hesitate to do occassional cooking with the kids: make spaghetti, grow alfalfa sprouts and make a salad, fix favorite recipes with them, etc. The Health Department won't bother you on that sort of thing.

Don't overlook the fact that wherever you have a large group of people you have the potential for starting a food buying club — a "food conspiracy" or "food buying co-op." For complete information on how to do this, write to:

Office of Economic Opportunity

Washington, D.C. 20506

Ask them to send you the booklets GREEN POWER, and HOW TO ORGANIZE A CO-OP.

OR, write to:

Last Gasp Echo-Funnies Company

P.O. Box 212

Berkeley, California 94704

Ask them to send you: EATER'S DIGEST: HOW HILLGRAS FOOD CONSPIRACY IS RUN. Although the booklet is free, and very nicely done, I'd suggest sending a donation. I'm sure they'd appreciate it.

In California, for more info you can phone:

Food Conspiracy Switchboard

415-845-9627

OR:

People's Architecture

415-548-3661

The money your group might save on food can help offset the cost of running the school. Together, the school and the food conspiracy can become the centers of focus for a strong community. Well worth considering!

MISCELLANEOUS BOOK LIST

1. *Big Rock Candy Mountain,* Portola Institute, 1115 Merrill Street, Menlo Park, CA 94025 (a periodical) $3.00
2. *This Magazine Is About Schools,* 56 Esplanade Street East, Suite 301, Toronto 215, Ontario, Canada (a periodical)
3. *Teacher Drop-Out Center,* P.O. Box 521, Amherst, Mass. 01002
4. *Summerhill Society,* 6063 Hargis St., Los Angeles, CA 90034 and also at 339 Lafayette St., New York, New York 10012
5. *World Game,* Design Department, Southern Illinois University, Carbondale, Illinois 62901
6. *Rasberry Exercises,* Rasberry & Greenway, Freestone $3.95
7. *The Underground Guide To The College of Your Choice,* Susan Berman, N.A.L. $1.50
8. *Environment,* Committee for Environmental Information, 438 North Skinker Blvd., Saint Louis, Mo. 63130 (a periodical)

15

PUBLISHER'S PAGE

The public school systems in this country run on political juice. City and county taxes provide money, the state legislature provides money, policy and administration to make the system go. An outsider — say a student or a parent — can't change anything in the system except by exerting contrary political juice, and plenty of it. Plenty of political juice most people don't have. An example of the first law of politics: change and political juice usually exist together in inverse proportion. So the folks who don't like what passes for 'education' in their school district are frustrated.

Then there are other folks. They feel that the primary service the public school system provides is a kind of sociable, supervised babysitting for most of the working day. But these people aren't too happy with the quality of the supervision. They feel that too much regimen and authoritarianism makes their children either dull and bored or anxious and insecure. So they'd like to see changes too.

Still other folks disavow both the quality of public school education and the need for the babysitting service. They are trying to simplify their lives and at the same time become more self-reliant. They point out that public education in this country is a by-product of the industrial revolution — a convenient *city* technique for freeing more people to work the machines. And since these folks are trying to free themselves from dependence on the city, they naturally reject city techniques. To them, learning by doing is the answer.

Among the first group of people there is the greatest unrest, and they apply the greatest pressure for change on the system. To the second group goes credit for the 'open classroom' or, how to make public babysitting endurable. The third group of people go out and start their own schools — the 'new schools' or 'free schools' — often in defiance of everybody.

We're siding more with the third group of folks, and hope in this book we give you enough tools that you will be able to take back control of your children's destiny, and turn your frustration toward joy.

16

HOW I CAME TO WRITE THIS BOOK

PERSONAL STUFF ABOUT ME AND MY FAMILY

I first became interested in education while tramping around Mexico in 1961. A friend and I took a train from the States to Mexico City, then hitchhiked south to Acapulco. Finding Acapulco too expensive for our limited budgets, we boarded a bus, along with a dozen natives, a crate of chickens, two goats and a man carrying a five gallon jug of "agua puro," and made our way over the mountain to a small coastal settlement called "Pie de la Questo." We stayed there nearly three weeks, becoming friendly with the children who hustle tourists: the Chicklet vendors and the *musicos.* Most of them were eight to ten years old, and came to us to learn American slang.

The children already knew a little straight English but the words they picked up on the beaches often got them in trouble. For example, one boy thought "chickenshit" meant "Senorita." The day before we arrived he caused quite a stir when he addressed the leader of a tour-group of middleaged women as "chickenshit." So his interest in learning was not in the least abstract, but was rooted in his need to solve simple problems. His ignorance of the language undoubtedly cost him customers. Because of these things, he proved to be a ready student.

When I returned to the States and to college, I often thought about my Mexican teaching experience, and soon began to attend classes in the Education Department on campus. But they never made much sense to me. Still, my interest in teaching grew, and after graduation I took a job with a small private school, where I was to teach English, History and Social Science to grades one through six.

The pay was terrible. As I recall, I took home $260 a month. But at that point, the opportunity to teach was my reward. There was a devil in paradise, though; the principal was a rigid authoritarian who believed firmly in memorization and drill. Luckily, she was a busy woman who spent little time at the school.

From the very beginning I believed that learning was only possible when the subject to be taught came from the student's desire to know; when it was not imposed arbitrarily by the teacher's lesson plans. This simple principle, learned on the beaches of Mexico, remains at the core of my teaching philosophy.

I was never attracted to teaching in the public schools, though I felt no particular animosity toward them, either. I visited public school classrooms from time to time, exploring possibilities for teaching, and what were called "innovative new approaches" and always found them tiring. Many of the children seemed bored and even anxious, while those pointed out by the teacher as "excellent students" seemed to me dull and obedient.

When I could not find a teaching position that interested me, I earned my living as a carpenter. From time to time I volunteered as a teacher's aide in one of the more progressive private schools in San Francisco. When my son, Nathan, was born, we equipped part of our apartment as a nursery school and took in four children whose mothers worked during the day. Nathan's mother had a deep respect for children in their efforts to cope with, enjoy, and learn to understand their worlds.

In 1966, I found my way into the Children's Centers, which in California are administered by the Department of Education and provide daycare for the children of working parents throughout the state. I was drawn to them because they had no defined educational structure, and so seemed to have real potential for learning. In many ways the Children's Centers were far ahead of the public schools. In the last few years, for example, the public schools have begun to adopt the "open classroom" approach to teaching which has been common to the Centers for twenty years. "Open classroom" generally means that children are free to move around as they wish — not confined to their chairs — and are free to choose among the various educational activities available in the room.

My students at the Children's Center ranged in age from five to twelve. They split their time away from home between the Center and public school, but were with us about three hours a day. We were teachers, surrogate parents, and just plain friends with joy, sympathy, love, indifference and irritation coming in more or less equal quantities throughout the day.

I left San Francisco to set up and supervise a Children's Center in Marin County across the Bay. In my two and a half years in Marin, I began to see more of what was happening in the public schools, which I had the opportunity to visit at one time or another.

At the same time, Aaron, my second wife's son, began to have trouble in school. It was not that he wasn't bright; he got good grades in most subjects.

Nor was he a "discipline problem;" he was awarded a "good citizenship" certificate at the end of first grade. The problem was that he was learning to distrust his own resources, and to become dependent on the teacher's judgement of his performance as a measure of his worth, trusting her judgement before he'd trust his own. Here are two examples of what I mean:

FIRST: The class was being taught a complex phonics system which the teacher called "Reading." Although Aaron couldn't grasp the phonics (which was created by educators to make learning to read easier) he still could read as well as any other child his age (six years old). He believed that because he couldn't grasp the phonics, that he couldn't and never would, learn how to read. After I got him to understand that phonics and reading were two different things, he began to renew his interest in reading.

SECOND: At home Aaron is taught to speak up for himself, and to express his wants clearly and directly. But while standing in line to get a drink of water, his teacher swatted him with a ruler for talking. (The rigidity there is inhuman, but that's almost secondary.) When I asked Aaron what he said, he told me, "I said, 'Billy, you can't take cuts.'" A second teacher witnessing the scene confirmed that this was true. Aaron was confused, and wanted to know who was right: him or the teacher. I told him that he was. If a child learns nothing else, I believe that he should learn to exercise and trust his own judgement.

Soon after the second incident which I list here, we took Aaron out of school. I wrote a long letter to the district Superintendent of Schools. In the letter I said that my wife and I were taking Aaron out of school, explained why we were doing so, and said that we were not interested in working with the schools in any way, since our experience had already shown that we could not change the situation in time to benefit our own child. I made fifty copies of this letter which I mailed to every teacher on the staff at Aaron's school, his principal, and local politicians. Copies also went to the Governor and to the State Superintendent of Schools. After I mailed the letters, my wife started to get nervous. She anticipated phone calls from officials, and people coming to visit. But as it turned out, the silence was deafening. There was not a single response to the letter, nor did anyone from the school ask where Aaron was after he did not show up for school the rest of the year.

Linda and I both had anxieties about taking Aaron out of school. Turn to page 101, "Questions and Answers" for a discussion of some of the more universal ones. Furthermore, we didn't have the money to send him to a private school, and there were no available "free schools" in our community. We decided that our only answer was to educate him at home; his mother and I would be his teachers.

In the first weeks that he was out of school, Aaron, Linda and I set up work spaces for him in the house. There was a table where he did his "academic work," and another in Linda's studio, where he could paint and do other art work. We made a place to keep books for his school work, and another for crayons, paints, and other art materials. From this beginning came the ideas for MINIMAL SCHOOL ONE (page 24) and "working by the clock" (page 95).

In that first year out of school, Aaron had no one his own age with whom to share his learning experiences. However, there are a large number of children his own age in the neighborhood where we live, and so he was not without friends. Furthermore, the social order of the neighborhood children is far richer and more complex than the community of children supervised by adults in his former public school, and from the neighborhood experience he was able to explore and develop skills for dealing with social systems. We think he is confident and adept in his relationships with children in his own peer group.

One thing has become clear to me. There are a great many families who are discontent with the public schools, and are searching for the tools to build alternatives. Although there are an increasing number of books available on the subject of alternative schools, none of them deals with simple facts, like what forms you must fill out and how to get them. None tell exactly what the relationships between compulsory education laws and registering your educational operation with the school authorities are. None tell how to handle the myriad of hassles which must be resolved in order to survive as a school.

At the time that I was researching and writing the book, I was also putting together my own school, and so the experience of actually doing this became central to the writing. Like my first students on the beach in Mexico, my interest in learning continues to be rooted in the need to solve real problems directly related to my day to day existence.

17

FORMS AND DOCUMENTS

THIS SECTION CONTAINS

The documents in this section will give you a clear picture of the red tape which you will have to deal with to become an "approved" private school. You'll find the following here:

California State
Department of Education
Form No. R-4 (Replaces Form No. BP-5)

Return the completed form to the office of the county superintendent of schools by October 15, 1971, for transmittal to the State Department of Education.

PRIVATE SCHOOL AFFIDAVIT
Required by California Education Code Section 29009.5

This form is for reporting information required from private schools. Sections 12154 and 29009.5 of the California Education Code are printed on the attached sheet, together with appropriate instructions. A single *affidavit* may be submitted for two or more schools administered as a unit; however, directory, enrollment, and other data on the reverse of this form should be prepared separately for each school. Reproduce the reverse side of this form as necessary to supply one copy for each school in operation.

I. SCHOOL NAMES AND ADDRESSES. List every name, real or fictitious, under which this private school has done and is doing business in California, as well as every address of such school.

Name_____   Name_____

Street address_____   Street address_____

City_____ ZIP_____   City_____ ZIP_____

(Use an additional sheet of paper for additional names and addresses.)

II. DIRECTORS AND PRINCIPAL OFFICERS

1. Name_____ Position_____

   Street address_____ City_____ ZIP_____

2. Name_____ Position_____

   Street address_____ City_____ ZIP_____

3. Name_____ Position_____

   Street address_____ City_____ ZIP_____

(Use an additional sheet of paper for additional names.)

III. SCHOOL RECORDS. The following records are maintained at the address stated, and are true and accurate:

Location address_____ City_____ ZIP_____

1. The records required to be kept by Section 12154, California Education Code.
2. The courses of study offered by the institution.
3. The names, addresses, and educational qualifications of the faculty.

IV. CERTIFICATION. *I hereby certify, under penalty of perjury, that to the best of my knowledge and belief the statements contained herein are true and accurate.*

Signature of owner or head_____ Date_____

Type or print name_____ Position_____

Private School Directory Data. A directory will be published as required by California Education Code Section 29009.5. Please indicate here the desired directory listing for your school; prepare separate data for each school currently in operation and for each address, duplicating this side of the form as necessary.

Please type or print.

Name of school_____ Telephone _____
(Include area code.)

Street address_____ Grades maintained_____

City_____ ZIP code_____ County_____

Owner or administrator_____ Position_____

- -

name and address of school

Enrollment on October 1

	1970	1971
Elementary		
Kindergarten	_____	_____
Grade one	_____	_____
Grade two	_____	_____
Grade three	_____	_____
Grade four	_____	_____
Grade five	_____	_____
Grade six	_____	_____
Grade seven	_____	_____
Grade eight	_____	_____
Ungraded	_____	_____

(check)

1. Type of school: Coeducational   _____

   Boys only   _____

   Girls only   _____

2. Period of operation:

   Opened this year   _____

   Completed one year   _____

   Completed two years   _____

   Completed three years or more   _____

High school

	1970	1971
Grade nine	_____	_____
Grade ten	_____	_____
Grade eleven	_____	_____
Grade twelve	_____	_____
Ungraded	_____	_____

3. If school is church-related, indicate denomination:

   Catholic   _____

   Episcopal   _____

   Hebrew   _____

   Lutheran   _____

   Seventh-Day Adventist   _____

   Other (specify) _____

Total enrollment   _____   _____

Graduates, grade twelve, 1970-71 year   _____

4. Are boarding facilities available?

   Yes__ No__

Special Education

This school offers special education programs for the following:

5. Is this school operated on a nonprofit basis?

   Yes__ No__

(check)

6. Total number of teachers on the staff: _____

Physically exceptional pupils:

7. Name of public school district in which the school is located:

   Visually handicapped   _____

   Aurally handicapped   _____

   _____

   Orthopedically handicapped   _____

8. Person preparing this form, to whom questions may be directed:

   Multihandicapped   _____

   Other (specify) _____

   Name _____

Mentally exceptional pupils:

   Mentally retarded   _____

   Title _____

   Educationally handicapped   _____

   Gifted   _____

   Telephone _____
   (Include area code.)

   Other (specify) _____

EMERGENCY INFORMATION CARD   (SIDE 1)

To be filled out by parents and filed in the principal's office.

_____   _____   _____
    Student's name   Sex   Birthdate

_____   _____
    Student's home address   Home phone

_____   _____
    Parent's name   Address

_____   _____ _____
    Mother's employer   Address   Phone

_____   _____ _____
    Father's employer   Address   phone

                                              (SIDE 2)

In case of emergency, when we the parents or guardian cannot

be reached, you are hereby authorized to take appropriate

actions for obtaining professional services and arranging

necessary transportation. Alternative person to be called:

1. _____
        Name   Address   Phone

2. _____
        Name   Address   Phone

Physician to be called: 1st choice_____
                                        Name   Phone

                        2nd choice_____
                                        Name   Phone

Parent's signature_____Date_____

STANDARD HEALTH FORM FOR SCHOOLS

PHYSICIAN'S REPORT FOR SCHOOL USE   Date......................

Pupil's name... Birth date...........................
       (LAST)   (FIRST)   (MIDDLE)

Address... Phone...............................
      (STREET)   (CITY)

School attending .... Grade...............................

School address...
      (STREET)   (CITY)

Parent's Authorization

I hereby give my consent to the school named above to receive from or send to Dr. .... an
information concerning my child.

....
     SIGNATURE OF PARENT   ADDRESS

Reason for this referral:...

HISTORY OF IMMUNIZATIONS AND TESTS

	Date or age last given				Date or age last give
DPT (initial series completed)		Polio: Salk			
Boosters for DPT..............			(1)	(2)	(3)
DT (initial series completed)........		Sabin..............			
Boosters for DT..............			(1)	(2)	(3)
Smallpox..............		Tuberculin test ...... Pos. .. Neg.			
Reaction		Chest x-ray ...... Pos. ... Neg. ...			
Other (specify)					

1. Is this pupil subject to any condition for which the school should make special preparation; e.g., epilepsy, fainting, diabetes, heart disease, etc.?	Recommendations
2. Is there any emotional, mental or physical condition for which this pupil should remain under periodic medical observation?	Recommendations
3. Does the pupil have asthma, eczema or other allergies, including drug allergies?	Comments
4. A. Is there any known vision or hearing problem for which the school should compensate by proper seating or other action? B. Is there need for a special visual or hearing examination?	Recommendations
5. Does the pupil wear any dental appliances? What was the date of the last dental examination?	Recommendations
6. Is there a health problem which limits participation in: A. Classroom activities? B. Physical education? C. Competitive athletics (indicate sports)?	Recommendations
7. Is this pupil under your regular care?	Yes No How long?

8. Other comments or recommendations: ....

....
   DATE OF EXAMINATION   SIGNATURE OF EXAMINING PHYSICIAN

....
         ADDRESS

DOCTOR: PLEASE RETURN THIS FORM TO SCHOOL
(Health Form 2.6A-Revised 9/63)

CALIFORNIA STATE DEPARTMENT OF EDUCATION
Legal Office
Sacramento, California

STATE DEPARTMENT OF EDUCATION
721 CAPITOL MALL
SACRAMENTO, CALIFORNIA   95814

Superintendent of
Public Instruction

SUMMARY OF CERTAIN OF THE LAWS OF CALIFORNIA RELATING TO THE ESTABLISHMENT AND MAINTENANCE OF PRIVATE SCHOOLS, PARTICULARLY THOSE OF KINDERGARTEN, ELEMENTARY, AND SECONDARY GRADES

This summary does not include reference to every law pertaining to the establishment or maintenance in California of private schools. It does not contain the exact language of the laws referred to. Its purpose is to call attention to laws most frequently made the subjects of inquiry.

1. ESTABLISHMENT

(a) **Jurisdiction of Department of Education**

The State Department of Education lacks jurisdiction over the establishment of private schools except that:

(1) **Diploma and Degree Granting Institutions.** Private schools which propose to issue any diploma, certificate, transcript, document or other writing in any language other than a degree representing that any person has completed any course of study beyond high school, unless such school comes within one of the exceptions set forth in subdivisions (b), (c) or (d) of the Education Code Section 29007 or those exceptions contained in Education Code Section 29002 or 29002.1, must secure annually from the Superintendent of Public Instruction authorization to issue any of the aforesaid documents.

Except for those schools accredited pursuant to Section 6060 (g) (1) and (2) of the Business and Professions Code (Education Code Section 29007.1), private schools may not issue any degree, academic degree, technological or honorary degree, or title signifying satisfactory completion of the requirements of an academic educational, or professional program of study beyond secondary school level, including a recognized honorary title conferred for some meritorious recognition, unless such school meets the requirements of any one of the three subdivisions of Subdivision (a) of Education Code Section 29007.*

(2) **Correspondence Courses:** Any person, either on his own behalf or as the representative of any privately conducted correspondence school or of

---

*FOOTNOTE: A copy of Chapter 1 of Division 21 of the Education Code and regulations issued pursuant thereto will be sent on request.

118

any private person, firm, association, partnership, or corporation whatsoever, who, by personal contact, in California, solicits the sale of or solicits and sells any correspondence course of study beyond high school or high school level, or below high school level, for a remuneration or other consideration to be provided for such courses, is required by Education Code Section 29007.3 to hold a valid permit to engage in such activities issued by the State Board of Education or the Superintendent of Public Instruction by virtue of authority delegated to him by the State Board of Education. If no permit is held, any such correspondence course contract is voidable at the option of the purchaser. An application on a prescribed form, an application fee of $15, and a bond are required.**

(3) **Course of Education.** Education Code Section 29007.5 provides that any adult course leading to an educational technological, professional, or vocational objective, must be approved by the State Superintendent of Public Instruction and no diploma or honorary degree shall be issued or conferred unless such approval is obtained, except if given by a parochial or denominational school, or by a person or entity that has met the requirements of other sections of Division 21 of the Education Code or if offered solely for avocational or recreation purposes. The criteria for approval are set out in Education Code Section 29007.5.

(4) **Identification of Outstanding Students.** The State Board of Education may provide for the identification of students with outstanding aptitudes and ability in private schools under a State Plan approved by the U.S. Commissioner of Education under Title V of the National Defense Education Act of 1958 (Education Code Section 30103). Upon request of a private school maintaining any grade 7 through 12, the State Board of Education may contract with the school for such testing (Education Code Section 30102).

(5) **Reporting Information to Superintendent of Public Instruction.** "29009.5. Every person, firm, association, partnership, or corporation offering or conducting private school instruction on the elementary or high school level shall between the 1st and 15th day of October of each year, commencing on October 1, 1967, file with the Superintendent of Public Instruction an affidavit or statement, under penalty of perjury, by the owner or other head setting forth the following information covering the preceding fiscal year:

(a) All names, whether real or fictitious of the person, firm, association, partnership, or corporation under which is has done and is doing business.

(b) The address, including city and street, of every place of doing business of a person, firm, association, partnership, or corporation within the State of California.

(c) The address, including city and street, of the location of the

**FOOTNOTE: A copy of Education Code Section 29007.3 will be sent on request.

records of the person, firm, association, partnership, or corporation, and the name and address, including city and street, of the custodian of such records.

(d) The names and addresses, including city and street, of the directors, if any, and principal officers of the person, firm, association, partnership, or corporation.

(e) The school enrollment by grades, number of teachers, co-educational or enrollment limited to boys or girls and boarding facilities.

(f) That the following records are maintained at the address stated, and are true and accurate:

(1) The records required to be kept by Section 12154

(2) The courses of study offered by the institution.

(3) The names and addresses, including city and street, of its faculty, together with a record of the educational qualifications of each.

Whenever two or more private schools are under the effective control or supervision of a single administrative unit, such administrative unit may comply with the provisions of this section on behalf of each of the schools under its control or supervision by submitting one report.

Filing pursuant to this section shall not be interpreted to mean, and it shall be unlawful for any school to expressly or impliedly represent by any means whatsoever, that the State of California, the Superintendent of Public Instruction, the State Board of Education, the California State Department of Education, or any division or bureau thereof, or any accrediting agency has made any evaluation, recognition, approval, or endorsement of the school or course unless this is an actual fact.

The Superintendent of Public Instruction shall prepare and publish a list of private elementary and high schools to include the name and address of the school and the name of the school owner or administrator."

(b) **Jurisdiction of Department of Public Health**

Schools or other establishments, other than private business schools or colleges, providing special services, including schooling, for physically handicapped persons must be licensed by the Department of Public Health (Health and Safety Code Sections 1500-1517).

(c) **Concurrent Jurisdiction of Public Agencies**

Both the State Department of Social Welfare or a city or county inspection service approved by that Department (Welfare and Institutions Code Sections 16000-16015) and the appropriate public school authority (Education Code Sections 12154 et seq.) have equal responsibility for examining and determining the nature of places where children under 16 years of age are kept and educated and each must perform the duties imposed upon it by law, independently of the other. An instititution which is primarily a school may also be an institution for the reception and care of children and is subject to the laws relating to each. If an institution gives some children board and lodging and proper educational instruction as a school, the institution is, for such children, a school. If, however, the institution cares for other children for whom it did not render complete or proper educational instruction, but rather cares for them as an institution within the Welfare and Institutions Code, it must be inspected and licensed by the State Department of Social Welfare. A private institution which is in fact a school that provides its pupils with entirely inadequate instruction but is otherwise a school of satisfactory character, must be dealt with as provided in Education Code Sections 12451-12455. (Attorney General's Opinion NS 5393, 3 Ops. Cal. Atty. Gen. 191.)

2. ALL SCHOOLS – OPERATION, PREMISES, EQUIPMENT

(a) Fire Safety, Health, Sanitation –All Schools

There are certain requirements with respect to fire safety and to health and sanitation which schools, in common with other enterprises, must meet, but which are outside the scope of this summary.

Inquiries relating to fire safety should be addressed to the State Fire Marshal. (See Appendix A for address.)

Inquiries relating to health and sanitation should be addressed to the State Department of Public Health (see page 10 for address) or to the county health officer of the county in which the school is to be established.

It is suggested that inquiry be made of the city clerk of the city, if any, and the county clerk of the county in which a school is to be maintained to determine what city or county ordinances need to be met with respect to the establishment and conduct of a private school.

(b) School Premises–Access Gates–All Schools

The governing authority of a private school which is on land entirely enclosed by walls or fences must provide access gates of sufficient size to permit entrance of public ambulances, police equipment, and fire fighting equipment, and if the gates are to be locked, the locking devices must be designed to permit entrance by the use of chain or bolt cutting devices. (Education Code Section 12081)

(c) School Equipment–All Schools

(1) **Fire Alarm System.** The authorities of every private school must equip every school building having an occupant capacity of 50 or more students or containing more than one classroom, with a dependable and operative fire warning system and must provide for the sounding of a fire alarm signal upon the discovery of fire and not less than once each calendar month in the following manner except that when the fire alarm system used has a distinctive tone and is used for no other purpose, the manner of sounding the signal may be different:

When the signal is given by means of an apparatus emitting intermittent sound signals, the signal shall be given by repeated successive short intermittent signals for a full period of ten (10) seconds, to be immediately followed by an intermission or period of silence of five (5) full seconds before the signal is repeated.

When the signal is given by means of an apparatus emitting prolonged or continuous sound signals, the signal shall be given by prolonged whistle blast or other sound signal continuously sounded for a full period of ten (10) seconds, to be immediately followed by an intermission or period of silence of five (5) full seconds before the signal is repeated.

In no case shall the signal be given for less than a one-minute period, and then only in the manner indicated. (Education Code Sections 12001-12005)

(2) **First Aid Kit.** The authorities of every private school must equip the school with a first aid kit which must be taken on any field trips by the person in charge of the pupils on the trip. Every first aid kit shall include the following articles and such other equipment as the school officials charged with the duty of maintaining it may consider useful or necessary for such purpose:

(A) 12 3" x 3" sterile gauze packages

      4 1" gauze roller bandages

      4 2" gauze roller bandages

      4 Triangular bandages

      1 Roll adhexive tape 1" (10 yds.)

(B) An American Red Cross first aid textbook or written instructions for use of contents of the first aid kit.

(C) Whenever a field trip is conducted into an area which is commonly known to be infested by poisonous snakes, the first aid kit shall include a snake bite kit. (Education Code Section 11951-11955)

(3) **School Buses.** With certain exceptions motor vehicles carrying school pupils at or below the 12th grade level to or from a private school or private school activities are school buses subject to Vehicle Code Sections 2807, 2808, and 25257. (Vehicle Code Section 545)

(4) **Eye Protective Devices.** The authorities of every private school must equip the school with industrial quality eye protective devices, as defined in Education Code Section 12092, and require them to be worn in courses when an individual is engaged in, or observing, an activity or using hazardous substances likely to cause injury to the eyes. Some of those activities and substances are listed in Education Code Section 12091. (Education Code Sections 12090-12094)

3. PUPILS – ALL SCHOOLS

(a) **Prohibition Against Giving Out Information Concerning School Pupils**

Personal information and access to written records concerning particular minor students may not be given or shown to any person except to the persons and under the circumstances described in Education Code Section 10751. (42 Ops. Cal. Atty. Gen. 195) See also Education Code Section 10751.5 on release and use of names and addresses of pupils in the 12th grade.

(b) **Prohibition Against Hazing**

The hazing of private school pupils is a misdemeanor. (Education Code Section 10852)

(c) **Identification of Outstanding Students Grades 7 – 12.**
(See 1(a) (4))

(d) **Poliomyelitis and Measles Immunization Required Before Admission**
(H. & S. C. Sections 3380–3387 and 3400–3407) (See 3400 H. & S. C. for numerous exceptions to measles immunization.)

(e) Discontinuance of attendance of, or denial of admission to, a physically handicapped, mentally retarded or multiply handicapped child otherwise subject to the compulsory education law must be reported to the county superintendent of schools.

4. GENERAL REQUIREMENTS FOR SCHOOLS ATTENDED BY CHILDREN BETWEEN AGES 6 and 16

(a) **Time.** A private school attended by children between 6 and 16 years of age in lieu of their attendance upon a public school, must be a full-time day school. (Education Code Section 12154) A private school, to be exempt from the state compulsory education law must obtain verification by the attendance supervisor of the school district that it has filed its annual affidavit with the State Superintendent of Public Instruction in compliance with the requirements of Education Code Section 29009.5. (Education Code Section 12154)

A private school attended by a minor under Education Code Section 12154 in lieu of otherwise required attendance upon a public full-time day school, is not required to be maintained for the minimum school day required of public schools by Education Code Sections 11001 – 11008, 11051 – 11054, and 11061 nor is it required to be maintained for not less than 175 days in each school year, except as otherwise provided in Education Code Section 17553, as are public schools under Education Code Section 17551. The term "half day or more," as used in Education Code Section 12154 with respect to absence from attendance upon a private full-time day school, means one-half or more of the full-time day of the particular private school. (Attorney General's Opinion NS 5413; 3 Ops. Cal. Atty. Gen. 257.)

(b) **Teachers**

The school must be staffed by teachers capable of teaching. (Education Code Section 12154) In determining whether a person employed in a private school is "capable of teaching" as required by Education Code Section 12154, the standards to be used should be comparable to those required for public school teachers excepting only as to the holding of credentials (Attorney General's Opinion NS 3965).

(c) **Records of Attendance**

The attendance of the pupils must be kept by the authorities of the private school in a register, and the record of attendance must indicate clearly every absence of the pupil from school for a half day or more during each day that school is maintained during the year. (Education Code Section 12154)

The State School Register for Public Elementary Schools furnished by the State Superintendent of Public Instruction to public elementary school teachers under Education Code Section 13558 may be sold by the Department of Education to private elementary schools if the Department of Education finds the use of the Register in private schools will be of benefit to public employees in checking private elementary school attendance under and for the purposes of Education Code Sections 12451–12454, and 12401–12413. (Attorney General's Opinion NS 4918)

(d) **Language in Which Teaching Is Done**

English is a basic language of instruction, however, the governing board of any school district and any private school may give instruction bilingually. Bilingual instruction is authorized to the extent that it does not interfere with the systematic sequential and regular instruction of all pupils in the English language. (Education Code Section 71). (Certain exceptions for mentally gifted pupils Education Code Section 12154.5 and for certain children who are proficient in a foreign language, Education Code Section 71.)

(e) **Report of Severance of Attendance of Pupil**

If a county board of education so provides by regulation, a private school must report to the county superintendent the severance of attendance of a pupil between ages 8 and 18, whether by exclusion, expulsion, exemption, transfer, suspension, beyond 10 days or other reason. (Education Code Section 12103)

5. REQUIRED COURSES OF STUDY

(a) **Courses Required by Virtue of Education Code Section 12154**

Education Code Section 12101 calls for compulsory public school education for children between ages 6 and 16 years. Section 12154 exempts those children who are being instructed in a private full-time day school and provides that such schools shall offer instruction in the several branches of study required to be taught in the public schools of the State.

Paragraphs (1) to (5) below list those subjects required to be taught in all elementary and secondary public schools and hence in all private schools, attended by children between 6 and 16 years of age.

(1) Public safety and accident prevention at appropriate grade levels (Education Code Section 8503).

(2) The nature of alcohol, narcotics, restricted dangerous drugs, and dangerous substances (Education Code Section 8504).

(3) Fire prevention (Education Code Section 8503).

(4) Protection and conservation of resources (Education Code Section 8503).

(5) The effects of alcohol, narcotics, drugs, and tobacco upon the human body (Education Code Section 8503).

(6) In addition to the subjects listed in paragraphs 1 through 5, the branches of study required to be taught in grades 1 through 6 and to be

offered in grades 7 through 12, in the public schools, and, therefore, in private schools attended by children between 6 and 16 years of age in those grades, are shown in the following charts.

Grades 1 – 6 (Education Code Section 8551)

Subject	Grade In Which Instruction Is Required					
	1	2	3	4	5	6
English	X	X	X	X	X	X
Mathematics	X	X	X	X	X	X
Social Sciences	X	X	X	X	X	X
Science	X	X	X	X	X	X
Fine Arts	X	X	X	X	X	X
Health	X	X	X	X	X	X
Physical Education	X	X	X	X	X	X

Such other studies as may be prescribed by the governing board.

Grades 7 – 12 (Education Code Section 8571)

The course of study must offer courses in the following areas of study: English, foreign language*, social sciences**, physical education***, science, mathematics, fine arts, applied arts, driver education, and such other studies as may be prescribed by the governing board.

*Beginning not later than grade 7 (Education Code Section 8571(c).

**Instruction in social science must include early California history and a (EI study of the role and contribution of the various ethnic groups (Education Code Section 8553).

***Certain students may be exempt from physical education (Education Code Section 8703).

Requirements for High School Graduation

No pupil shall receive a diploma of graduation from grade 12 who has not completed the course of study and met standards of proficiency prescribed by the governing board. Requirements shall include: English, American history, American government, mathematics, science, physical education, and such other courses as may be prescribed (Education Code Section 8573).

6. SCHOOLS ATTENDED BY CHILDREN BETWEEN AGES 16 and 18

A private full-time day school, attended by children between 16 and 18 years of age who otherwise would be required to attend in public schools, is not required to meet any specific standards or requirements except such as are otherwise noted. Privately maintained "part-time classes" attended by children between 16 and 18 years of age who otherwise would be required to attend compulsory continuation classes maintained by a school district, must be "satisfactory." To be exempt from compulsory continuation education a private school must obtain verification by the attendance supervisory of the school district that the private school has complied with the provisions of Education Code Section 29009.5 requiring annual filing of an affidavit of prescribed information with the Superintendent of Public Instruction. (Education Code Section 12551.5)

STANDARD LEASE AGREEMENT

This Indenture made the _____ day of _____ one thousand nine hundred and _____

Between _____
hereinafter called "lessor_____", and
_____ hereinafter called "lessee _____",

Witnesseth: That the said lessor _____ do _____ by these presents, demise and lease unto the said lessee _____, and the said lessee _____ do _____ hereby hire and take from the said lessor _____,
(description and location of the property)

with the appurtenances, for the term of _____
commencing on the _____ day of _____ 19 _____, and ending on the _____ day of _____ 19 _____, both days included, at the _____ rent or sum of _____ dollars, payable in lawful money of the United States of America _____ in advance, in manner following, to wit:
(time and manner of monthly payments)

And it is hereby agreed that if any rent shall be due and unpaid, or if default shall be made in any of the covenants herein agreed to be kept by the lessee _____, then it shall be lawful for the said lessor _____, at _____ option, subject, to the giving of such notice, if any, as shall be required by law, to termiate this lease and to re-enter the said premises and remove all persons therefrom.

And the said lessee _____ do _____ hereby covenant, promise, and agree to pay to the said lessor _____ the said rent in the manner herein specified, and not to assign this lease, or let or underlet the whole or any part of said premises, without the written consent of lessor _____, and that, at the expiration of said term, the said lessee _____ will quit and surrender the said premises in as good state and condition as reasonable use and wear thereof will permit (damages by the elements excepted). Should the lessee _____ hold over the term herein created, such tenancy shall be from month to month only, and be on the same terms and conditions as are herein stated.

And the said lessor _____ do _____ hereby covenant, promise, and agree that the said lessee _____ paying the said rent and performing the covenants aforesaid, shall and may peaceably and quietly have, hold, and enjoy the said premises for the term aforesaid.

ARTICLES OF INCORPORATION
OF
(NAME) INCORPORATED
A NON-PROFIT CORPORATION

FIRST:

The name of this corporation shall be (name), incorporated.

SECOND:

The purposes for which this corporation is formed are:

A. The specific and primary purpose is to create, establish, and provide an independent non-profit educational resource for the advancement of education and for scientific purposes, in order that improved ways of assisting children in their learning and development can be explored, demonstrated, and implemented.

B. The general purposes for which this corporation is formed are to operate exclusively for scientific and educational purposes.

C. This corporation shall have and exercise all rights and powers conferred on corporations under the laws of the State of _____, provided, however, that this corporation is not empowered to engage in any activity which in itself is not in furtherance of its purposes as set forth in subparagraph (A) and (B) of this article second.

THIRD:

This corporation is organized pursuant to the general non-profit corporation law of the state of _____, and does not contemplate pecuniary gain or profit to the members thereof and it is organized for non-profit purposes.

FOURTH:

The county in this state where the principal office for the transaction of the business of this corporation is located is _____ county.

FIFTH:

A. The powers of this corporation shall be exercised, its properties controlled, and its affairs conducted by a board of directors. The number of directors herein provided for may be changed by a by-law duly adopted by the members.

B. The names and addresses of the persons who are appointed to act as the first directors are:

NAME	ADDRESS
_____	_____
_____	_____
_____	_____

SIXTH:

The persons who are the directors (or trustees) of this corporation from time to time shall be its only voting members and on ceasing to be a director (or trustee) of this corporation, any such person shall cease to be a voting member.

In the election of directors (or trustees) each member of this corporation shall be entitled to one vote for each office to be filled.

The voting members and directors (or trustees) of this corporation shall have no liability for dues and assessments.

SEVENTH:

The authorized number of qualifications of members of the corporation, different classes of membership, if any, the property, voting and other rights and privileges of members and their liability to dues and assessments and the method of collection thereof, shall be set forth in the by-laws.

EIGHTH:

The property of this corporation is irrevocably dedicated to scientific and educational purposes meeting the requirements for exemption provided by Section 214 of the Revenue and Taxation Code, and no part of the net income or assets of this corporation shall ever inure to the benefit of any private persons, upon the dissolution or winding up of the corporation, its assets remaining after payment of, or provision for payment of, all debts and liabilities of this corporation, shall be distributed to a non-profit fund, foundation, or corporation which is organized and operating exclusively for scientific and educational purposes meeting the requirements for exemption provided by Section 214 of the Revenue and Taxation Code, and which has established its tax exemption status under Section 501 (c) (3) of the Internal Revenue Code.

If this corporation holds any assets in trust, or the corporation is formed for charitable purposes, such assets shall be disposed of in such manner as may be directed by decree of the Superior Court of the County in which the corporation has its principal office, upon petition therefor by the Attorney General or by any person concerned in the liquidation, in a proceeding to which the Attorney General is a party.

NINTH:

This corporation shall not carry on propaganda or otherwise attempt to influence legislation and this corporation shall not participate in or intervene in any political campaign (including the publishing or distribution of statements) on behalf of any candidate for public office.

TENTH:

It shall be the operational policy of this corporation not to discriminate against any person on the basis of race, color, religion, creed, or national origin, including but not exclusive of nondiscriminatory admissions of students and members, and equal use of all facilities.

ELEVENTH:

At no time during the existence of this corporation shall Article Eighth or Article Eleventh hereof be amended other than by resolution being first adopted by the unanimous vote of the then board of directors and approved by the vote or written consent of all the then members of the corporation.

128

The undersigned, being the persons herein above named, as the first directors, have executed these articles of incorporation the _____ day of _____, 197_.

_____
Incorporator

_____
Incorporator

_____
Incorporator

NOTARY PUBLIC CERTIFICATE

STATE OF   )
                               SS,
COUNTY OF   )

On _____ before me, the undersigned, a notary public in and for the state of _____, personally appeared _____

_____

_____ known to me to be the person _____ whose name _____ subscribed to the within instrument and acknowledged that _____ executed the same.
    WITNESS my hand and official seal.

Signature _____

_____
Name (Typed or Printed)

(THIS AREA FOR
OFFICIAL NOTARIAL
SEAL)

BY-LAWS
OF
(NAME), INCORPORATED

I
Principal Office

The principal office for the transaction of the business of the corporation is fixed and located at _____ (City), _____(County), _____ (State). The board of directors may at any time or from time to time change the location of the principal office from one location to another in this county.

II
Membership

Section 1. Members

There shall be two classes of members of this corporation. The first class of members shall be known as voting members who shall be the acting directors and each shall have one vote. The second class of members shall be known as associate members and shall have no vote.

Section 2. Qualifications of Associate Members

Any person who contributes funds or other property to this corporation shall be an associate member of this corporation unless he is, or becomes, a voting member of this corporation. Election of a person as a voting member of this corporation shall terminate his membership as an associate member of this corporation.

Section 3. Annual Meeting

The annual meeting of the members of this corporation shall be held on the _____ ((E.g.,) second Tuesday of June) of each year at _____ _.m. at the principal office of this corporation, or at any other time in _____ ((E.g.,) June) and at any other place determined by a resolution of the board of directors. No notice of any such annual meeting need be given if it is held on the _____ ((E.g.,) second Tuesday of June) at _____ _.m. at the principal office of the corporation; otherwise written notice of the time and place of the annual meeting shall be delivered personally to each voting member or sent to each voting member by mail or other form of written communication, charges prepaid, addressed to him at his address as it is shown on the records of the corporation. Any notice shall be mailed or delivered at least five days before the date of the meeting.

Section 4. Special Meetings

Special meetings of the members of the corporation for any purpose or purposes may be called at any time by the president of the corporation or by any _____ (Number) directors.

Written notice of the time and place of special meetings of the members shall be given in the same manner as for annual meetings of the members.

The transactions of any meeting of the members of this corporation, however called and noticed, shall be as valid as though had at a meeting held after regular call and notice if a quorum is present, and if, either before or after the meeting, each of the voting members not present signs a written waiver of notice, or a consent to holding this meeting, or an approval of the minutes of the meeting. All the waivers, consents, or approvals shall be filed with the corporate records or be made a part of the minutes of the meeting.

Section 5. Quorum

A quorum for any meeting of the members shall be _____ (Number) voting members.

III
Board of Directors

Section 1. Number of Directors

The board of directors shall consist of _____ (Number) members until the number of directors is changed by amendment to these by-laws.

Section 2. Quorum

_____ (Number) members of the board of directors shall constitute a quorum for the transaction of business.

Section 3. Powers of Directors

Subject to limitations of the articles of incorporation, other sections of the by-laws, and of _____ (State) law, all corporate powers of the corporation shall be exercised by or under the authority of, and the business and affairs of the corporation shall be controlled by, the board of directors. Without limiting the general powers, the board of directors shall have the following powers:

(a) To select and remove all the other officers, agents, and employees of the corporation, prescribe such powers and duties for them as may not be inconsistent with law, the articles of incorporation, or the by-laws, fix their compensation, and require from them security for faithful service.

(b) To conduct, manage and control the affairs and business of the corporation, and to make rules and regulations not inconsistent with law, the articles of incorporation, or the by-laws.

(c) To borrow money and incur indebtedness for the purposes of the corporation and for that purpose to cause to be executed and delivered, in the corporate name, promissory notes, bonds, debentures, deeds of trust, mortgages, pledges, hypothecations, or other evidence of debt and securities.

Section 4. Election and Term of Office

Except as provided below for the initial terms of the first directors, the term of office of each director of this corporation shall be _____ (Number) years or until his successor is elected. Successors for directors whose terms of office are then expiring shall be elected at the annual meeting of the members in the year such terms expire. A director may succeed himself in office.

Section 5. Vacancies

Vacancies in the board of directors shall be filled by a majority of the remaining directors then in office even though less than a quorum, or by the sole remaining director. A successor director so elected shall serve for the unexpired term of his predecessor.

Section 6. Place of Meeting

Regular meetings of the board of directors shall be held at any place, within or without the state, that has been designated from time to time by resolution of the board or by written consent of all members of the board.

Section 7. Organization Meeting

Immediately following each annual meeting of members, the board of directors shall hold a regular meeting for the purposes of organization, election of officers, and the transaction of other business. No notice of such organizational meeting need be given.

Section 8. Other Regular Meetings

Other regular meetings of the board of directors shall be held without call on the _____ ((E.g.,) second Tuesday) of each _____ ((E.g.,) April, July, and October) at _____ __.m.; provided, however, that should that day fall on a legal holiday _____ (or a Saturday or Sunday), then the meeting shall be held at the same time on the next day that is not a _____ (Saturday, Sunday, or) legal holiday. No notice need be given of any regular meeting.

Section 9. Special Meetings

Special meetings of the board of directors for any purpose or purposes may be called at any time by the president or by any _____ (Number) directors.

Written notice of the time and place of special meetings shall be delivered personally to each director or sent to each director by mail, charges prepaid, addressed to him at his address as it is shown on the records of the corporation. The notice shall be mailed at least _____ (Number) days before the time of the holding of the meeting.

The transactions of any meeting of the board of directors, however called and noticed and wherever held, shall be as valid as though had at a meeting held after regular call and notice, if a quorum is present and if either before or after the meeting each of the directors not present signs a written waiver of notice or a consent to hold the meeting or an approval of the minutes.

Section 10. Action Without a Meeting

Any action by the board of directors may be taken without a meeting if all members of the board individually or collectively consent in writing to this action. Such written consent or consents shall be filed with the minutes of the proceedings of the board.

Section 11. Removal

A director may be removed from office, for cause, by the vote of a majority of the directors.

Section 12. Compensation

The directors shall receive no compensation for their services as directors.

IV
Officers

Section 1. Officers

The officers of this corporation shall be a president, vice president, secretary, and treasurer, and such other officers as the board of directors may appoint. One person, other than the president, may hold more than one of these offices. Officers other than the president need not be members of the board of directors.

Section 2. Election

The board of directors shall elect all officers of the corporation for terms of _____ (Number) year(s), or until their successors are elected and qualified.

Section 3. Vacancies

A vacancy in any office because of death, resignation, removal, disqualification, or otherwise shall be filled by the board of directors.

Section 4. President

Subject to the control of the board of directors, the president shall have general supervision, direction, and control of the business and affairs of the corporation. He shall preside at all meetings of the members and directors, and shall have such other powers and duties as may be prescribed from time to time by the board of directors.

Section 5. Vice President

In the absence or disability of the president, the vice president shall perform all the duties of the president and in so acting shall have all the powers of the president. The vice president shall have such other powers and perform such other duties as may be prescribed from time to time by the board of directors.

Section 6. Secretary

The secretary shall keep a full and complete record of the proceedings of the board of directors, shall keep the seal of the corporation and affix it to such papers and instruments as may be required in the regular course of business, shall make service of such notices as may be necessary or proper, shall supervise the keeping of the records of the corporation, and shall discharge such other duties of the office as prescribed by the board of directors.

Section 7. Treasurer

The treasurer shall receive and safely keep all funds of the corporation and deposit them in the bank or banks that may be designed by board of directors. Those funds shall be paid out only on checks of the corporation signed by the president, vice president, treasurer, or secretary or by such officers as may be designated by the board of directors as authorized to sign them. The treasurer shall have such other powers and perform such other duties as may be prescribed from time to time by the board of directors.

V

Amendment of By-Laws

These by-laws may be amended or repealed and new by-laws adopted by the vote of a majority of the members of the board of directors at any directors' meeting, except that a by-law fixing or changing the number of directors may be adopted, amended, or repealed only by the vote or written consent of a majority of the members of the corporation or the vote of a majority of a quorum at a meeting of the members called for that purpose and which is the vote of the majority of those present and voting.

VI

Non-discrimination Policy

It shall be the operational policy of this corporation not to discriminate against any person on the basis of race, color, religion, creed, or national origin, including but not exclusive of nondiscriminatory admissions of students and members, and equal use of all facilities.

STATE AND FEDERAL EXEMPTION APPLICATIONS ARE MUCH ALIKE
THIS IS THE FEDERAL APPLICATION

FORM **1023** (Rev. April 1965)	U.S. TREASURY DEPARTMENT—INTERNAL REVENUE SERVICE **EXEMPTION APPLICATION** *(To be made only by a principal officer of the organization claiming exemption)*	To be filed in duplicate with the District Director for your District.

For use of organizations applying for exemption under section 501(a) and described in section 501(c)(3) of the Internal Revenue Code, which are organized and operated **(or will operate)** exclusively for one or more of the following purposes (check purpose(s)):

☐ Religious ☐ Charitable ☐ Scientific ☐ Testing for Public Safety
☐ Educational ☐ For the prevention of cruelty to children or animals ☐ Literary

Every organization that claims to be exempt must furnish the information and data specified in duplicate. If any organization fails to submit the information and data required, this application will not be considered on its merits and the organization will be notified accordingly.

This application shall be open to public inspection in accordance with section 6104(a)(1) of the Internal Revenue Code. See separate instructions for Form 1023 to properly answer the questions below.

1a. Full name of organization	b. Employer identification number

2. Complete address (number, street, city or town, State and Postal ZIP code)

3a. Is the organization incorporated? ☐ Yes ☐ No	b. If "Yes," in which State and under which law (General corporation, not for profit, membership, educational, eleemosynary, etc.)? Cite statutory provisions.

4a. If not incorporated, what is form of organization?	b. Date incorporated or organized	c. Month and day on which the annual accounting period ends

5a. Has organization filed Federal income tax return(s)? ☐ Yes ☐ No	b. If "Yes," form number of return filed and Internal Revenue District where filed.	c. Year(s) filed

6. After July 1, 1950, did the creator of your organization (if a trust), or a contributor to your organization, or a brother or sister (whole or half blood), spouse, ancestor, or lineal descendant of such creator or contributor, or a corporation controlled directly or indirectly by such creator or contributor, enter into any of the transactions (or activities) enumerated below? NOTE: If you have any knowledge or contemplate that you will be a party to any of the transactions (or activities) enumerated in 6a through 6f, check **"planned"** in the applicable block(s) and see instructions.

	Yes	No	Planned		Yes	No	Planned
a. Borrow any part of your income or corpus?				d. Purchase any securities or other property from you?			
b. Receive any compensation from you?				e. Sell any securities or other property to you?			
c. Have any part of your services made available to him?				f. Receive any of your income or corpus in any other transaction?			

	Yes	No
7. Have you issued or do you plan to issue membership, stock, or other certificates evidencing voting power in the organization?		
8a. Are you the outgrowth or continuation of any form of predecessor(s)?		
b. Do you have capital stock issued and outstanding?		
c. Have you made or do you plan to make any distribution of your property to shareholders or members?		
d. Did you receive or do you expect to receive 10 percent or more of your assets from any organization, group of affiliated organizations (affiliated through stockholding, common ownership, or otherwise), any individual, or members of a family group (brother or sister whether whole or half blood, spouse, ancestor, or lineal descendant)?		
e. Does any part or will any part of your receipts represent payment for services of any character rendered or to be rendered by you?		
f. Are you now, have you ever been, or do you plan to be engaged in carrying on propaganda, or otherwise advocating or opposing pending or proposed legislation?		
g. Do you participate or plan to participate in or intervene in (including the publishing or distributing of statements) any political campaign on behalf of or in opposition to any candidate for public office?		
h. Have you made or do you plan to make any payments to members or shareholders for services rendered or to be rendered?		
i. Does any part or do you plan to have any part of your net income inure to the benefit of any private shareholder or individual?		
j. Are you now or are you planning to be affiliated in any manner with any organization(s)?		
k. Do you hold or plan to hold 10 percent or more of any class of stock or 10 percent or more of the total combined voting power of stock in any corporation?		

9. Has any State or any court (including a Court of Probate, Surrogate's Court, etc.) ever declared whether you were or were not organized and operated for charitable, etc., purposes? ☐ Yes ☐ No. If "Yes," attach copies in duplicate of pertinent administrative or judicial decisions.

10. You must attach copies in duplicate of the following:

a. If incorporated, a copy of your articles of incorporation, or if not incorporated, a copy of your constitution, articles of association, declaration of trust, or other document whereby you were created setting forth your aims and purposes, a copy of all amendments thereto, and any changes presently proposed.

b. A copy of your bylaws or other similar code of regulations, all amendments thereto, and any changes presently proposed.

c. A complete statement of assets and liabilities as of the end of each annual accounting period (or as of the date of the filing of this application, if you were in existence for less than a year).

d. A statement of receipts and expenditures for each annual accounting period of operation (or for the period for which you were in existence, if less than a year).

e. A statement which clearly indicates what State statutes or court decisions govern the distribution of assets upon dissolution. (This statement may be omitted if your charter, certificate, or other instrument of organization makes provision for such distribution.)

f. A brief statement of the specific purposes for which you were formed. (Do not quote from or make reference to your articles of incorporation, constitution, articles of association, declaration of trust, or other document whereby you were created for this question.)

g. A statement explaining in detail each fund-raising activity and each business enterprise you have engaged in or plan to engage in, accompanied by copies of all agreements, if any, with other parties for the conduct of each fund-raising activity or business enterprise.

h. A statement which describes in detail the nature of each of your activities which you have checked on page 1, activities which you sponsor, and proposed activities.

i. A statement which explains fully any specific activities that you have engaged in or sponsored and which have been discontinued. Give dates of commencement and termination and the reasons for discontinuance.

j. A statement which describes the purposes, other than in payment for services rendered or supplies furnished, for which your funds are expended or will be expended.

k. A schedule indicating the name and position of each officer, director, trustee, etc., of the organization and the relationship, if any, by blood, marriage, adoption, or employment, of each such person to the creator of the organization (if a trust), to any person who has made a substantial contribution to the organization, or to a corporation controlled (by ownership of 50 percent or more of voting stock or 50 percent or more of value of all stock), directly or indirectly, by such creator or contributor. The schedule shall also indicate the time devoted to position and compensation (including salary and expense account allowance), if any, of each officer, director, trustee, etc., of the organization.

l. A copy of each lease, if any, in which you are the lessee or lessor of property (real, personal, gas, oil, or mineral) or in which you own an interest under such lease, together with copies of all agreements with other parties for development of the property.

SIGNATURE AND VERIFICATION

Under penalties of perjury, I declare that I have examined this application, including accompanying statements, and to the best of my knowledge and belief it is true, correct, and complete.

Date	Signature of officer	Title

FORM 1023 (REV. 4-65)

EMPLOYER'S TAX GUIDE:
HOW TO PAY WAGES THE RIGHT WAY

One way to explain the process is to start with the forms, all available from your friendly IRS, and describe the function of each. Thus:

Form SS-4: Every employer must have an "Employer Identification Number." This form is your application for that number, and is your first step toward becoming a full-fledged employer.

Form SS-5: Every employee must also have a number, this being his Social Security number. In the event that you hire someone who does not already have a S.S. number, this form would be his application for one.

Form W-4: This is the little form on which the employee reports how many dependents he claims for payroll deductions.

Form 941: Contains all information about the money the employer has withheld from wages, and must be filed each: April 30, July 31, Oct. 31, and Jan. 31.

Form 501: Known as the "Federal Tax Deposit Form" it accompanies the employer's deposit of withheld taxes in the Federal Reserve Account. Filed quarterly, as is Form 941.

Form 940: Must be filed if employer is paying Federal Unemployment Tax. (You're exempt if your school is a non-profit corporation.)

Form 508: Another "Federal Tax Deposit Form," this one for depositing Federal Unemployment Taxes, again on a quarterly basis, the same as Form 941.

Form W-2: What the employer must send to the employee at the end of each year to go along with the employee's yearly tax returns. Briefly, what happens is this: the employer withholds certain taxes from his employees' wages, keeps records of these withholdings, and deposits these withholdings, plus other money in some cases, in Federal Reserve Accounts.

Federal Unemployment Tax, and Social Security Taxes, can both be withheld in a similar manner. But if your school establishes its non-profit status (see page 00), you may be exempt from these withholdings. Otherwise, you deduct these taxes as follows:

Social Security: 5.2% of employee's earnings paid from employee's pocket.

Federal Unemployment Tax: Employer pays 3.2% of employee's earnings. Admittedly, a lot of work, but once you get the whole thing together, it ain't half bad. Don't forget about the "Dome Payroll Book" (page 00) which has easy-to-follow instructions for doing all of the above. Remember, employees of non-profit organizations are exempt from paying Social Security and Federal Unemployment Taxes, but they are NOT EXEMPT from Federal Income Taxes.

INDEX

To The Reader:

Writing a book is very much a one-sided affair. I'd enjoy hearing from you — your complaints, your praise, suggestions you might have for improving the book, questions you might want answered about schools, or whatever. I'll answer everything I can. Write to me:

Hal Bennett
c/o The Bookworks
1409 Fifth Street
Berkeley, CA 94710